GALATIANS
—— *and* ——
1 & 2 THESSALONIANS

Text copyright © John Fenton 1996, 1999

The author asserts the moral right
to beidentified as the author of this work.

Published by
The Bible Reading Fellowship
Peter's Way, Sandy Lane West
Oxford OX4 5HG
ISBN 1 84101 012 X

First edition (Galatians) 1996
Revised edition 1999
10 9 8 7 6 5 4 3 2 1 0

Acknowledgments
Unless otherwise stated, scripture quotations are taken from
the New Revised Standard Version of the Bible, Anglicized
Edition, copyright © 1989, 1995 by the Division of
Christian Education of the National Council of the
Churches of Christ in the United States of America, and are
used by permission. All rights reserved.
Revised English Bible with the Apocrypha copyright ©
1989 by Oxford University Press and Cambridge University
Press.
A catalogue record for this book is available
from the British Library.

Printed and bound in Great Britain
by Caledonian Book Manufacturing International, Glasgow

GALATIANS
—— *and* ——
1&2 THESSALONIANS

THE PEOPLE'S
BIBLE COMMENTARY

JOHN
FENTON

A BIBLE COMMENTARY FOR EVERY DAY

▶ The Bible Reading Fellowship
OPENING THE BIBLE

Introducing the
People's Bible Commentary
Series

Congratulations! You are embarking on a voyage of discovery—or rediscovery. You may feel you know the Bible very well; you may never have turned its pages before. You may be looking for a fresh way of approaching daily Bible study; you may be searching for useful insights to share in a study group or from a pulpit.

The People's Bible Commentary (PBC) series is designed for all those who want to study the scriptures in a way that will warm the heart as well as instructing the mind. To help you, the series distils the best of scholarly insights into the straightforward language and devotional emphasis of Bible reading notes. Explanation of background material, and discussion of the original Greek and Hebrew, will always aim to be brief.

- If you have never really studied the Bible before, the series offers a serious yet accessible way in.

- If you help to lead a church study group, or are otherwise involved in regular preaching and teaching, you can find invaluable 'snapshots' of a Bible passage through the PBC approach.

- If you are a church worker or minister, burned out on the Bible, this series could help you recover the wonder of scripture.

Using a People's Bible Commentary

The series is designed for use alongside any version of the Bible. You may have your own favourite translation, but you might like to consider trying a different one in order to gain fresh perspectives on familiar passages.

Many Bible translations come in a range of editions, including study and reference editions that have concordances, various kinds of special index, maps and marginal notes. These can all prove helpful in studying the relevant passage. The Notes section at the back of each PCB volume provides space for you to write personal reflections, points to follow up, questions and comments.

Each People's Bible Commentary can be used on a daily basis, instead of Bible reading notes. Alternatively, it can be read straight through, or used as a resource book for insight into particular verses of the biblical book.

If you have enjoyed using this commentary and would like to progress further in Bible study, you will find details of other volumes in the series listed at the back, together with information about a special offer from BRF.

While it is important to deepen understanding of a given passage, this series always aims to engage both heart and mind in the study of the Bible. The scriptures point to our Lord himself and our task is to use them to build our relationship with him. When we read, let us do so prayerfully, slowly, reverently, expecting him to speak to our hearts.

Contents

PBC GALATIANS: INTRODUCTION

Some time in the middle first century AD this letter from Paul was brought by a messenger to be read to the Christian communities that Paul had established in Asia Minor (modern Turkey).

We know enough from the letter itself and from other early Christian writings to understand much of what Paul is saying. But there are some questions to which we do not know the answer. We do not know for certain where Paul was when he wrote to the Galatians, or where exactly they lived. Nor do we know how many churches there were, to which he sent the letter.

We can work out to some extent how the situation that provoked it had come about, although there is still much uncertainty about this. But we can understand enough of what Paul is saying in the letter to realize that it was, and still is, a document of the greatest importance.

The letter will have been read out in full, from beginning to end, in each community. This would not have taken long—probably less than one hour. You would find it a useful preliminary to the study of this book on Galatians to put yourself in the same position as its first recipients by reading the letter straight through from beginning to end at one sitting. It does not matter which translation you use, but the one quoted in this book is the New Revised Standard Version 1989 (NRSV). The abbreviation REB refers to the Revised English Bible (1989). As you read, remember that the divisions into chapters and verses which we are so familiar with in our printed Bibles were not invented until many centuries later.

There will of course be a vast difference between what the first recipients of the letter heard, and what we shall hear. They knew what the situation was that moved Paul to write to them—but we do not. Not until we have pieced together (from what Paul says in this letter and his other letters) what it was that had happened.

One thing will become clear immediately Paul's words are read. There was a row going on, and Paul is angry with some of those to whom he is writing. He addresses them as 'you foolish Galatians!' (3:1). There are some whom he does not name but against whom he utters threats: 'Let that one be accursed!' (1:8–9). Somebody has been saying things in Galatia and Paul is amazed that his converts have listened to them and begun to practise what was preached.

The row is about how one should live as a Christian; and that depends on what one believes about God and about what he requires of Christian people.

This may seem surprising, because the events we are concerned with happened within less than thirty years of the crucifixion and resurrection of Jesus in Jerusalem (which was probably in about AD30).

Some of the original followers of Jesus were still alive and Paul had met them. He refers to them in this letter as people about whom the Galatians will not need any further explanation and calls them simply 'James and Cephas [i.e. Peter] and John' (2:9).

We might think that at a time so close to its founder the church must have been united in faith and love. This letter shows that it was not so. There have been conflicts and disagreements in the history of Christianity from as far back as we can go.

It is not surprising that Jesus is quoted by Matthew as saying, 'Do not think that I have come to bring peace to the earth; I have not come to bring peace, but a sword' (10:34). This sword divided the followers of Jesus from those who did not believe in him and also divided the followers themselves into rival groups. The letter to the Galatians is firsthand evidence for the absence of peace from among Christians in the middle of the first century.

The Galatians themselves, of course, knew who their troublemakers were and what they had said. We can be fairly sure what it was they said but less certain who they were.

The main point of their message to the Galatians concerned what we call the Old Testament. But in those days those writings would have been referred to as 'the scriptures' or 'the scripture' (3:8, 22 and 4:30) or 'the law' (4:21). At the time when Galatians was written, the 'scriptures' involved in the dispute were the sacred books of the Jews, available to Greek-speaking readers in a translation known as the Septuagint. Neither the four Gospels nor any other Christian writings that we have now were in existence then, except possibly some earlier letters of Paul (e.g. 1 Thessalonians).

The opponents of Paul were saying that all Christians, whether they had been Jews before they were converted or Gentiles, should accept the scriptures in the same way—as books that contained authoritative rules for believers without any adjustments or modifications.

If this view had been accepted it would have had far-reaching results. People who had not been brought up as Jews (but who through Paul's preaching had believed in God and Jesus and been baptized) would have had to become members of Israel by circumcision (if they were males) and to have kept the whole of the Law of Moses as set out in the first five books of the Bible. They would have had to refrain from eating food that was classed as unclean. They would have had to adjust their lives so that they did no work from Friday evening till Saturday evening in order that they might keep the sabbath every week. And there would have been a lot of other things as well.

We might think that such a message delivered to non-Jewish people would not have been popular. But we would be wrong. The evidence shows that the Galatians were thrilled with the idea of adopting these ancient customs. They were, they believed, sanctified by continuous practice that went back to the time of Moses and the exodus of the Israelites from Egypt—and even earlier than that, to Abraham and the patriarchs, as described in the early chapters of Genesis.

It is sometimes said that the first century AD was an age of anxiety in which many people felt rootless and insecure. But if you accepted the Law of Moses that would establish you as a member of an ancient people. You would have roots, and you could call Abraham your father and Sarah your mother. You would have an unrivalled genealogy and status, and you would belong to an institution that was more ancient than any competitor. You would be inside a privileged circle and no longer an outsider.

Paul says to the Galatians that 'You are observing special days, and months, and seasons, and years' (4:10)—which meant that they were observing the calendar of Jewish feasts and festivals. And they were not finding it a burden. Just the opposite. It was a delight and a benefit, a set of procedures that made them feel safe in a fast-changing world. If it had not been so, Paul would have had no need to write to the Galatians to tell them to stop it. Nor would he have been so angry with those who were promoting these ideas among the Galatian churches.

To first-century people who had not been brought up as Jews the idea of keeping the Law of Moses was very attractive—and so were the arguments that could be employed to persuade them to adopt this way of life. Our appreciation of Paul's letter will be greatly deepened if we can see what powerful and apparently irresistible arguments his opponents could call into service.

If we had been living in Galatia at the time, we might have been won over by Paul's opponents. We are immensely dependent on the benefit of hindsight. We know who won in the long run and what had happened to Christianity by the middle of the second century. Paul and his contemporaries did not. They could only weigh up arguments as they saw them at the time and to many people the arguments against Paul must have seemed irrefutable. They were straightforward and appealed to common sense whereas Paul's case must have appeared involved and unrealistic.

The opponents of Paul could say first of all that scripture was on their side. If the problem were raised in the form 'What must we do to belong to the people of God?', then the answer according to scripture was absolutely clear. God had told Abraham: 'Any uncircumcised male who is not circumcised in the flesh of his foreskin shall be cut off from his people; he has broken my covenant' (Genesis 17:14).

Both sides in the Galatian controversy appealed to scripture as the authority for what they were saying. But it cannot be denied that the opponents of Paul had the better claim to be doing what was clearly and unequivocally commanded in the Law.

These same opponents could have pointed out, secondly, that Jesus (and all the first disciples who had followed him in Galilee and Judea) had been circumcised. The circumcision of Jesus is recorded in only one of the four Gospels (Luke 2:21). But although that Gospel had not been written at the time of the controversy it would have been impossible to suppose that Mary and Joseph would not have seen to this on the eighth day after his birth, as the Law required. So if the founder of the movement and the foundation members had all kept the Law how could some later followers not do the same?

Thirdly, if one had asked at that time where authority was to be found and which church was the model for all other churches, there was only one possible answer: the church in Jerusalem. The eleven disciples had moved there from Galilee after the resurrection—perhaps because of the expectation that the Lord would come from heaven to Jerusalem for the last judgment, and therefore they would be nearer to the place where he would arrive: 'On that day his feet shall stand on the Mount of Olives, which lies before Jerusalem on the east' (Zechariah 14:4).

James the Lord's brother became the leader of the Jerusalem church (he is mentioned in Galatians 1:19; 2:9, 12), and they would all have been circumcised and observant Jews. By what sort of reasoning could one avoid the conclusion that what was right in Jerusalem was not right elsewhere? Theology and church practice could not be subject to geography. If the church at the centre kept the Law of Moses, so should the churches on the circumference. Gentile sinners, as Paul calls them (2:15), were the last people to say what was right and what was wrong.

Fourthly, although Galilee and Judea had large non-Jewish populations at the time of Jesus, there is very little evidence that he had had dealings with Gentiles. There had been the Syrophoenician woman (Mark 7:24–30) and the centurion (Matthew 8:5–13; Luke 7:1–10). But in both cases their non-Jewish status had been noted as exceptional and the cures had been performed at a distance. Jesus had not entered their houses. Moreover there were traditions that Jesus had sent the twelve disciples to Israel only, not to Samaritans and not to Gentiles (Matthew 10:5f.).

We can imagine arguments along the lines: 'If the Lord did not deal with Gentiles while he was with us in the flesh how can we possibly go against his practice now? Surely Gentiles must become Jews in order to be members of the people of God? We have the authority of the Lord's usual practice for this, and nothing he said ever contradicted it.'

This is the attitude of Peter as it is described in Acts 10 and 11. He and others regard association with Gentiles, and eating unclean food, as a new revelation from God—not as something the Lord had commanded before his death and resurrection.

Those who troubled the Galatians had still more arguments, had they needed them, which must have seemed persuasive to Paul's converts. All over the area where they lived, there would have been synagogues attended by local Jewish residents on Saturdays. Paul preached in them and built on traditions that the synagogues preserved. He expects his readers in Galatia to know about Abraham, Moses and the prophets. Though a Gentile could have associate-member status in the synagogue (i.e. be a God-fearer), one could not be a full member without keeping the commandments, particularly circumcision, the sabbath and the dietary laws.

The Jews would never have thought that these commandments would be changed or rescinded. They had fought a war in the second century BC (the Maccabean revolt) in order to maintain their right to do these things and they had won. Their ancestors had died fighting for this freedom and books about them were still being written in the first century AD. To say that these laws were now out of date was as much as to say that the martyrs had died to no purpose.

Or we can imagine an argument of this kind: 'Jesus commanded us to love. But how can we love the other members of the people of God without adopting their ways? Paul does this himself,' the argument would have gone on, 'and he admits it: When he is with Jews he lives as a Jew (1 Corinthians 9:20). We live with Jews here in Galatia. So shouldn't we live as Jews and accept their terms for admission to their community?'

Finally, we need to recall that no Christian in those days expected that history would still be continuing nearly two thousand years later. Both Paul and his opponents would have expected the Lord to return in their lifetime. 'We will not all die, but we will all be changed, in a moment, in the twinkling of an eye, at the last trumpet' (1 Corinthians 15:51–52). They were praying for the Lord to come and to come quickly. So it would seem odd to suppose that there should be separate and parallel arrangements for Christians who had been Jews and those who had been Gentiles.

There were, they thought, only a few years to run. Charity and convenience would both urge them in favour of a common lifestyle. It was the lifestyle of the patriarchs, the people of God in the past, and of Jesus and his apostles. It was also the lifestyle of the church in Jerusalem and those who had brought the 'full gospel' to Galatia in order to correct the errors of Paul—someone who had never known the Lord 'in the flesh' and who was a one-time persecutor of the faith.

Paul faced a barrage of excellent, knock-down arguments and it must have seemed as if his opponents had all the trumps. If we had been Galatians we would certainly have been impressed by their persuasiveness. What can Paul say to win us over to his side?

His method is selective. He never quotes Genesis 17:12–14, the passage that is so explicit on the permanence of the law concerning circumcision ('throughout your generations'). He quotes other parts of Genesis—from chapters 15, 16, 17 and 18—but not the passage concerning circumcision. If we had asked him how to explain this commandment he would probably have said that it was an ordinance that was intended to apply only until Christ came. Similarly, he never quotes words of Jesus explicitly in this letter. He never uses an argument in the form: 'The Lord said this, therefore we must do it.' He quotes scripture frequently, probably because his opponents were doing so and he had to do the same when he answered them. But his authority for saying what he believes is not based on scripture as theirs may have been. He interprets scripture in the light of a faith that depends on something else—and he uses the passages from the Old Testament to illustrate this faith.

He explains this in a letter to the Corinthians: 'Whenever Moses is read [to those who do not believe], a veil lies over their minds; but when one turns to the Lord, the veil is removed' (2 Corinthians 3: 15–16). Faith comes first and the interpretation of scripture depends on that.

What is the ground of Paul's faith? As we read this letter we notice again and again that Paul refers to a series of events that have taken place in the recent past—mainly in the previous twenty years or so. The birth of Jesus and his death and resurrection are the beginning of the series. The conversion of Paul, from being a zealous observer of the Law and persecutor of the church to being a preacher, comes next. His relations with the church in Jerusalem is also part of the series, and a particular incident when Peter was with Paul in Antioch.

Then there is Paul's first visit to the Galatians and the result of it—their faith in the gospel and what the Spirit did to them: 'Did you experience so much for nothing?' he asks them (3:4). Almost the last words of the letter draw attention once more to what has certainly happened. If they look at Paul's body they will see the marks left by the beatings he has received in the synagogues (6:17). These marks show that he preaches a message that angers those who keep the Law: 'Why am I still being persecuted if I am still preaching circumcision? In that case the offence of the cross has been removed' (5:11).

'Getting into a rut' is a common experience. We can see only a certain set of facts—and they all seem to point one way and to require only one conclusion. The person who can help those who are in this state is the one who can show that there are more facts to be taken into account; and that when this is done they point to a very different conclusion.

This is what Paul is doing, in his letter to the Galatians. He uses recent events that have occurred in the lifetime of many of his readers—the death and resurrection of Jesus, his own conversion from Judaism to Christianity, his encounter with the leaders of the

Jerusalem church and with the synagogues, and the origin and subsequent history of the churches in Galatia—to show that God is dealing with human beings in a different way now from how he had done in the past.

The result of this is that believers have a freedom that nobody had ever known before. If they would reflect on what had happened to them they would see that they had been brought into a new relationship with God and with one another that they had not enjoyed previously. It would be foolish to return to the state they were in before Paul had preached the gospel to them.

The permanent value of Paul's letter to the Galatians is that it reminds those who read it of the advantages they have as believers. The crucial point is not that they have come to know God but that God has come to know them (4:9).

The good news is always more than we can adequately retain. It has to be heard again and again, because its implications are always more than anyone can discern. In this letter, perhaps even more than in any other of his letters, Paul performs the task of recalling those who read it to further and further discoveries of the goodness of God towards them.

One final point may need to be made before we begin to read the text of Paul's letter in detail. Paul was dealing with a particular situation, in a particular place. He was not writing for all places and all times. It would therefore be possible to misunderstand what he wrote by taking it out of context—as though he had been speaking 'timeless truths'.

He wrote other letters, and some of them have survived. In 1 Corinthians, for example, we can see him providing instructions for congregations that were divided and confused; and he will quote the scriptures to them as laws that they must fulfil (e.g. 1 Corinthians 9:9). Similarly, he will quote instructions that go back to 'the Lord' i.e. Jesus Christ (1 Corinthians 9:14).

There have been Christians who have been totally against any kind of law. The term that describes them is 'antinomians'. Paul was not one of those. He believed that 'the whole law is summed up in a single commandment, "You shall love your neighbour as yourself" ' (Galatians 5:14 quoting Leviticus 19:18).

To the Jews of the first century AD the Law of Moses was a package that had to be accepted *in toto*, without making any distinctions (see, for example, James 2:10). Paul is selective: he believes that the commandments which distinguished Jews from other people are no longer to be observed. Later writers were to make distinctions to clarify this point: the moral laws were to be observed, not the ceremonial laws—the ritual instructions, the food laws, the calendar and so on.

We are extremely fortunate in having some excellent commentaries on this letter. There is one by Martin Luther, written in the sixteenth century, that shows how the rediscovery of Paul at that time affected Christianity in the West, producing the situation of which we all are heirs.

Among the more recent commentaries, two may be picked out for mention: that of H.D. Betz, *Galatians* (Fortress, 1979); and that of J. Ziesler, *The Epistle to the Galatians* (Epworth Press, 1992).

Of older commentaries, one stands out as exceptional. Although it is based on the Greek text it can be used by those who know no Greek: E. de Witt Burton, *A Critical and Exegetical Commentary on the Epistle to the Galatians* (T. and T. Clarke, 1921). He provides at the end of the exposition (p. 362) one of the best brief summaries of Galatians that has ever been written:

> *Though it was probably dictated rapidly, and was certainly composed under the stress of deep emotion, the six brief chapters of which it consists constitute one of the most important documents of early Christianity and one of the noblest pleas ever written for Christian liberty and spiritual religion.*

1

The AUTHORITY *of the* APOSTLE

If we had lived at the time of the Roman empire and been contemporaries of Paul we would not have signed letters at the end as we do now. We would have put our name at the beginning of a letter and it would have been the first word we wrote. This is a far more sensible way of writing letters than ours. What the reader wants to know first is whom the letter is from. There is no need to turn to the last page to find out, if the sender's name comes first. All the books of the New Testament that were originally letters begin in this way and so do the two letters that are quoted in Acts (15:23–29; 23:26–30). It was the standard procedure, used by Greeks, Romans and Jews.

Paul's letters would have been read out to the congregations to which they were addressed. So we would expect to hear the name of the writer first, then the name of the recipients (here, 'the churches of Galatia') and then a greeting (here, vv. 3–5).

What is unusual in this letter is that the sender tells his correspondents not just that he is 'Paul an apostle', but what that means in his case. He writes, he says, with the authority of God and of Jesus Christ whom God raised from the dead. He is addressing (as we shall find later) people who do not agree with him and his purpose is to make them change their minds.

He has heard that they have recently started on a course of action that he believes to be totally wrong, and his aim in this letter is to persuade them to perform a complete change of direction. Moreover, it is not simply that he thinks that they are totally mistaken. He is also convinced that what they are doing now is contrary to God's will and that he has God's authority to tell them so.

Finding the right way

It is, in fact, even stranger than that. Paul believes that he is himself part of the evidence that what the Galatian churches are now doing is a mistake. Paul's own history, his autobiography, is part of the letter, because it is an instance of the argument that he is developing. If his hearers will recall (as he will invite them to do, in chapters 1 and 2) his earlier life and the change that took place in it (his conversion) they will see that they have taken a wrong turn and that they must go back to the point where they left the right way.

Paul says what it was that they had failed to understand, and he puts it in the greeting that follows: 'grace and peace'. This is what the disagreement between Paul and the Galatians is all about: 'What is meant by God's grace (or favour) and how do we know that we have it?' 'How has God made peace with us?' Paul had already mentioned the resurrection of Jesus Christ from the dead (v. 1): that was part of the answer to the question 'How do we know about God's grace?' Now he refers to the other event by which they should have known grace and peace: the crucifixion, in which Jesus 'gave himself for our sins to set us free from the present evil age'.

The chief fault of the Galatians is that they have not yet realized the full significance of what Paul had said when he preached the gospel to them. They had believed (or so they thought) and they had been baptized. But the implications of what they were doing had been lost on them. That was why they had taken the wrong turning and why they would now have to go back.

Paul is telling them that he must recall them to the two elements that make up his gospel: Christ died for our sins and was raised for our justification.

We are 'set free from this present evil age'. This is the theme of this letter: freedom, release from prison, liberty. We are like people coming out of a dark place into the light, who can see nothing because daylight is dazzling. We grope for support, for something to hang on to. That was how it was in Galatia—and it provoked a letter from Paul that has been immensely influential throughout the history of Christianity.

PRAYER

Help us to understand your apostle and his letter.
He writes for everybody, because he knows us so well.
Show us how his gospel is good news for us.

The CHURCHES *of* GALATIA

This letter was sent to more than one church; how many there were in Galatia, we do not know, nor do we know by what means each of them would hear what was written. Did Paul send one copy to each place? Or was there only one copy, and did the person who carried it for Paul move on from one church to another? One thing we know for certain: the word 'church' meant something different to them from what it usually means to us.

No buildings were ever called churches in the first two hundred years of Christianity. Believers met in private houses; hence the references in the New Testament to the church in someone's house (Romans 16:5; 1 Corinthians 16:19; Colossians 4:15; Philemon 2). The word 'church' meant the people who met, not the building in which they met. The literal meaning of the word, which was not a Christian invention, was 'meeting', 'assembly', 'coming together'. Only much later was the word used to mean the place where the meeting was held; but this happened long after the time when the New Testament books were being written.

It is also the case that the word was used at first, by Christians, to refer to the local meeting of those who believed. There was one meeting in Thessalonica, which Paul calls 'the church of the Thessalonians', there was another in Corinth, which he calls 'the church of God which is in Corinth', In Galatia, however, there was more than one meeting; that is why Paul addresses them as 'the churches in Galatia', in the plural; and notice how he does the same with 'the churches of Judea' (1:22).

That is to say, people thought in the plural, of a number of churches (one here, one there, and others elsewhere) before they thought of the one church that came into existence in different places. It was only later that the idea that all churches were instances of the one church was arrived at.

For many people, this is probably how it still is. We experience a meeting of believers in one particular place, before we grasp the idea of the church as a whole. We begin with the local group; it is that that is most real to us. The one, holy, catholic and apostolic church is an abstraction.

Diversity can be difficult

Problems, of course, arise from this. Few congregations are happy to merge with other congregations. Loyalty is to the group we know and to the particular place where it meets. This is nothing to be ashamed of; rather, it is how we are, how we experience reality. We associate our experiences with the place where we have had them.

In one of his letters, Paul writes about his anxiety for all the churches—he says he is under daily pressure because of it (2 Corinthians 11:28). Each church had its own particular problems, needs, failures and successes. The churches were not identical, like clones. Paul could not have sent the letter to the Romans to Corinth, or Philippians to Thessalonica. But in the case of the Galatian churches he could; one letter went to them all, because all of them happened to be in the same situation.

PRAYER

Thank you for the variety of congregations.
Thank you for our local loyalties.
Thank you for Paul's care which helped to shape the young church.

3

TROUBLEMAKERS *in* GALATIA

Had we been used to receiving letters from Paul we should have expected that he would here have gone on to thank God for our faith and perseverance (this, like the opening, was standard practice in the Roman empire). We should therefore have been shaken rigid on hearing the next sentence read to us in one of the Galatian churches: 'I am astonished that you are so quickly deserting the one who called you.'

Instead of thanking God for us, he is expressing his amazement at our turning our backs on God—and on doing this so soon after we had received from God his greatest gift: his Spirit, that is, his life.

We have done this by listening to people who have preached a 'different gospel' from the one that Paul preached. But it is wrong to call it a gospel, or good news. It is, Paul knows, very bad news. We had been released from prison; but now we have voluntarily accepted another prison sentence. We have put our heads into a noose.

Paul is so angry that he pronounces an anathema (a curse) on whoever led us astray. And to make it completely clear he repeats it. He would not have been happy with the attitude, 'It doesn't matter what you think or believe; it's what you do that counts.' The Galatians have allowed their minds to think strange thoughts that they had never entertained before; and these new ideas have led them to do things that they had never done in the past: 'You are observing special days, and months, and seasons, and years' (4:10). Who have done this to the Galatians and what was it that they said?

Paul never names them in this letter. He had no need, because his readers knew exactly whom he was talking about. These people had come to Galatia (after Paul had moved on) as preachers of a gospel, and they claimed that they had greater authority than that of Paul. What they said in their preaching included the requirement that Gentile believers should keep the Law of Moses that was contained in the first five books of the Hebrew scriptures (Genesis to Deuteronomy).

We shall not understand Galatians unless we see that the preachers of the different gospel in Galatia had a most persuasive case. We might well have believed them rather than Paul. They could quote scripture. God told Abraham that circumcision was to be the sign of membership of God's people for ever: 'So shall my covenant be in your flesh an everlasting covenant' (Genesis 17:13, but see the whole chapter).

The Jewish martyrs who had died in the wars against the Greeks two centuries before had given up their lives rather than break the food laws by eating unclean meat (2 Maccabees 7). Jesus had been circumcised and had attended synagogue services. He had said that he had not come to abolish the Law or the Prophets (Matthew 5:17). The headquarters church of the Christian movement, in Jerusalem, was led by James the Lord's brother, and the family of Jesus were members of it (Acts 1:14). They all kept the Law. In any case, if charity 'beareth all things' should not the Gentile believers put up with some inconvenience in order to preserve the unity of the churches? Jesus had not made it clear whether his followers should cease to live as Jews.

Those who preached this other gospel were welcomed by the churches of Galatia: they were willing to keep the Law, beginning with the liturgical calendar. The troublemakers may have said (rightly or wrongly) that they came with the knowledge and authority of the church in Jerusalem to make up the deficiencies of the churches established by Paul. Paul, we shall see, emphasizes his independence of Jerusalem. He had no need of any human commission, because he was sent by God through Jesus Christ. People who came from James had caused trouble in Antioch (2:12) and it may have been similar preachers who had started the movement for keeping the Law in Galatia.

Quarrels among Christians and divisions between churches are not recent. Nor are they necessarily signs of our latter-day degeneration. They were there from the earliest Christian history. This letter may have been written within twenty-five years of the resurrection. Paul's letters to Corinth, Rome and Philippi also show the existence of groups among the churches who opposed one another—each claiming that it alone had the true gospel. God limits himself to what we can manage. He deals with us through human beings. His witnesses are flesh and blood and they are not without sin. They retain their ambitions, their quarrelsomeness, and their fear of people with ideas different from their own. All their insights are partial and imperfect.

PRAYER

Forgive us our trespasses. Thank you for accepting us as we are.
Do your will in spite of us.

The LIMITS of DIVERSITY

It has often been said that reading the New Testament letters (especially those written by Paul) is like listening to a telephone conversation when you can only hear what one party is saying. In order to make sense of what is going on you have to work out for yourself what the other person must have said, and it is always possible to make a mistake.

When Paul asks, rhetorically, 'Am I now seeking human approval?' he is probably replying to people in Galatia who were accusing him of acting merely in order to win popularity and support and saying that he lacked principles. They might well have had evidence (of a kind) to make such a charge against him, because Paul himself says that when he was with Jews he lived like a Jew and when he was with Gentiles he lived like a Gentile: 'I have become all things to all people.' He explains why: 'That I might by all means save some' (1 Corinthians 9:19–23).

Paul believed that the question of Jewish lifestyle was now a matter of the past and that it could be treated with indifference. All that mattered now was preaching the gospel and faith in God. He must preach, and he must do it in the way that he believed it had to be done—which was not how his opponents in Galatia were doing it. He believed that God had revealed to him the truth of the gospel and that God had appointed him as an apostle (that is, 'one sent') to preach this to the Gentiles.

Paul's missionary strategy

Paul had no choice in the matter. He was a slave of Christ and slaves had no freedom to choose. They had to do what they were told. So he is understandably angry that his missionary strategy of adopting the customs of those with whom he is living (over such matters as sabbath-observance, food regulations, attendance at synagogue and so on) is being interpreted as lack of principle and attributed to a low motive. They are using it as a stick to beat him and as a way of blackening his reputation in the churches that he has founded in Galatia.

'Am I now seeking human approval?' he asks. The letter that he is writing shows that this cannot be so. *Now*, in what he has just written in this letter, he has shown that there are limits to what can be approved of in the churches. His opponents have gone beyond the limits. That is why he has said, twice over for emphasis, 'let them be accursed!'

We often ask the questions: 'Where are the boundaries of the church?' 'What is the minimum that must be believed?' 'How do we know whether somebody is a Christian or not?' 'Are there tests for membership of the church?' The letter to the Galatians gives us one answer to these problems. Total contradiction cannot be legitimate. Paul gives an example in another letter; no one who was inspired by the Spirit could say both 'Jesus is Lord' and 'let Jesus be cursed!' (1 Corinthians 12:3); the first is the complete opposite of the second.

The same idea lies at the root of much of what he says here in this letter to the Galatians. Either God is dealing with us through the Law that he gave to Moses or he is not. Either we are right with God through keeping the Law (circumcision, food laws, sabbaths, etc.) or those things no longer matter.

As his letter proceeds we shall see more and more examples of this either/or method of argument. Paul, who was a large-hearted and intelligent and peace-loving person—even he could not find a way of containing in one community people who had totally opposite views; that is, both those who insisted that everybody keep the Law and those who believed that the former rules no longer applied. Later on, when he wrote to the Christians in Rome, he did his best to accommodate both sides. But that was because those who stood out for keeping the Law might, he hoped, no longer insist that others should do so.

In Galatia, he believes, there is less willingness on the part of the pro-Law troublemakers to come to any arrangement with the others, short of enforcing their total submission. Therefore, if that was their agenda, the only solution was to bar them from the churches. That is what this letter aims to do.

PRAYER

Let us not misrepresent those with whom we disagree.
Help us to see where we must take a stand.
Give us the courage to speak boldly when we should.

5 GALATIANS 1:11–12

GOSPEL MEANS MESSAGE

The word 'gospel' is important in this letter. Paul has already used it twice, in verses 6 and 7, and it will come seven times in all. There is also an associated word meaning 'to preach the gospel' and it comes six times. The words were characteristic of Paul—some of his favourite expressions. To us, 'gospel' suggests a book: the four Gospels, or the apocryphal Gospels of Philip, Thomas, and so on. But none of these had been written when Paul was using the word, so it would not have made the recipients of the letter think of a book. It meant a message. And not just any message, but one that you would be glad to hear. It meant good news.

In one of his later letters Paul will say more about the message. It is good news about Jesus, his death and resurrection and the significance of these events for everyone (1 Corinthians 15:3–5). He says there that he had received it and he must mean that he had received it from those who were believers before him. Here, however, he emphasizes something different: 'The gospel that was proclaimed by me is not of human origin; for I did not receive it from a human source.'

To the Corinthians he says he has received it. To the Galatians he says he had not. It looks as though he is contradicting himself. But that is not so. It is one thing to hear words spoken by human beings. It is something entirely different to believe what you hear. Believing requires more than simply hearing; faith comes from God.

The distinction between hearing and believing goes back to a passage in Isaiah that is quoted frequently in the New Testament:

> *Keep listening, but do not comprehend; keep looking, but do not under-*
> *stand. Make the mind of this people dull, and stop their ears, and shut their*
> *eyes, so that they may not look with their eyes, and listen with their ears,*
> *and comprehend with their minds, and turn and be healed.*
>
> *(Isaiah 6:9–10)*

Paul had been listening to what the followers of Jesus were saying for some time before he believed it for himself. That was why he had persecuted the church. He had thought that what they said was blasphemous, because it involved saying things about Jesus, a human being, that no good Jew could ever say. Paul changed from being a persecutor to being a follower—and the change was not the result of anything done by a human being. It was the work of God (see v. 15). God had shown Paul who Jesus was and what Jesus was doing. So though Paul had listened to people preaching the gospel he had not comprehended it. And though he had looked at the disciples he had not understood who they were. His understanding, comprehension and faith all came from God—not from a human source.

Conflict and fellowship

Galatians is about a conflict within the fellowship of Christ's disciples. Both sides of the conflict agree in some respects and disagree in others—and the disagreement runs very deep and has become extremely bitter. We have only Paul's side of the argument, and he is saying of anyone who opposes him from the other side, 'Let that one be accursed!' No doubt his opponents said the same of him. They agreed, however, on the events that constituted the gospel: Jesus had died, and God had raised him to life, and he had been seen after the resurrection. They agreed also that the scriptures had been fulfilled. Where they disagreed was over the implications of these things: was it now the case that Gentiles did not have to keep the Law of Moses in the way that Jews had done in the past?

Paul believes that his opponents in Galatia have not yet seen this necessary implication of the gospel—and he believes that it was God who revealed it to him. The trouble in Galatia was an example of a situation in which the Christian church sometimes finds itself. There is more to the gospel than we or our predecessors had thought. So perhaps there may be aspects of it still waiting to be perceived; implications not yet uncovered. The process of revealing the truth of the gospel to those who are already believers (but have not yet seen what is involved) is painful, both for those with insight and for those who lack it. There is no avoiding the pain.

PRAYER

Forgive our blindness and inertia.
Sustain our prophets and teachers.
Help us to comprehend and understand.

PAUL, *a* MAN SENT *by* GOD

At the beginning of the letter, Paul had said that he was an apostle 'sent neither by human commission nor from human authorities, but through Jesus Christ and God the Father' (v. 1). He returns to that, now, to show that this must be true. He is emphasizing it because there are people in Galatia who are saying that Paul must have received his authority from others—presumably, from the Jerusalem apostles. He must therefore be inferior to them. They would point to the fact that Paul had not been a follower of Jesus before the crucifixion, and they could argue from this that in any conflict between what the Jerusalem apostles said and what Paul said, they must be preferred; because they were superior to him. This is what Paul is disputing here. He and his message, he is saying, both come directly from Jesus Christ. The evidence for this is his autobiography.

There was a complete break in his life and a total change of direction. Up to a certain point he was going one way but after that he was going in the opposite way. He had disapproved of the followers of Jesus and tried to stamp the movement out. What motivated him at that time was zeal for the Law. He was a Pharisee—one of those who took the Law extremely seriously. (It should be noted that persecution of Jews by Jews was rare in the first century and that it would be a mistake to think of them as at all like Christians of later ages. Groups of Jews holding conflicting views, such as on resurrection, could co-exist side by side without resorting to violence.)

Then God intervened. Paul had thought that Jesus was a blasphemer who had rightly been executed by crucifixion and shown by the authorities to be cursed by God. He had also thought that the followers of Jesus participated in his error. Now, as a result of God's intervention, Jesus has been revealed to him as God's Son, his agent who does his Father's will. Paul also believed that he must preach this gospel to the Gentiles. In what order these ideas came to Paul he does not pause to tell us. The main point he wants to make is that this happened.

The persecutor became the apostle to the Gentiles—and it all happened without the intervention or assistance of any human beings. (Paul does not say anything about the part played by Ananias who is mentioned in Acts 9:10–19.) Paul did not go to Jerusalem—nor did he join any other group of believers. He went to Arabia—to preach—and then returned to Damascus, where his conversion had taken place. (See 2 Corinthians 11:32f. for Paul's account of his escape from Damascus. He was a wanted man because of what he was saying and he was already regarded as a troublemaker.)

Paul's autobiography stresses the intervention of God in his life. It was God who had 'set him apart before he was born' (compare Isaiah 49:1) and 'called him' (to be an apostle) 'through his grace' (not because he deserved it: he had been a persecutor. 'Grace' is another key word in this letter). Paul was a persecutor before he had contact with those 'who were already apostles before him'. There could not have been any opportunity for anyone to give authority to Paul—except God. The facts show that he is a man sent by God.

This passage underlines the priority of God in the life of Paul. The change of direction, from Pharisee to apostle, only makes sense if it is the action of God. And in the circumstances there was no one else involved. God acted alone. There is some sort of parallel to this kind of writing (theological autobiography) in the Old Testament prophets: Amos, Hosea, Jeremiah and Ezekiel all had initiatory visions which they record. A classic of this kind of writing, three hundred years later, is Augustine's *Confessions*, in which he shows how his life was directed and controlled by God. Writing of this sort seems to be characteristic of the Jewish-Christian tradition and to depend on a belief about God and his relationship with the individual believer.

Throughout this letter Paul will appeal to facts that could be checked: his conversion; his first visit to the Galatians; their faith and the gift of the Spirit; their freedom from previous restraints; the harvest of the Spirit; the marks on Paul's body, which showed that what he said was unacceptable to those who kept the Law of Moses.

Christianity is not simply a matter of faith. There is evidence—and some of this evidence is accessible to everybody. Believers have the testimony themselves. Loss of faith is a kind of self-contradiction.

PRAYER

Thank you for bringing us to this moment in our lives:
for everything that has led up to the present;
for those who have taught us and influenced us;
for gifts and graces freely given to us; for your knowledge of us.

Praise God *for* Paul

Paul continues to assert his independence. He was not instructed by anyone except God. He certainly wasn't instructed by the church in Jerusalem. The first time he went back there (after his conversion) was three years later, and he met Cephas, that is, Peter. (Paul refers to him more frequently by this Aramaic word, 'Cephas' meaning 'Rock', than by the Greek word 'Peter'.) He explains that he only stayed for a fortnight and that the only other apostle that he met was James, the Lord's brother, who seems to have become the leader of the Jerusalem church.

Paul insists, with an oath, that this is the truth—presumably because people were putting around a different story which implied that Paul had been instructed by the church in Jerusalem and that he was deviating from what he had been taught by them. No one else met him. They only heard that he had become a preacher of the gospel—and they gave thanks to God for him.

Paul skilfully puts key words that express his side of the argument into the mouths of the members of the Judean churches—people whom one might have expected to have been on the side of his opponents. They said that Paul was now 'proclaiming the faith'; literally, preaching as good news the faith he once tried to destroy. Paul makes them speak in his language and adds that they glorified God because of Paul. They, unlike his opponents in Galatia, realized that God was at work in Paul. If preaching the faith was a reason for glorifying God then, why is he being condemned for doing it now? Paul is claiming that the troublemakers lack consistency.

He says that for three years after his conversion he never went back to Jerusalem. Why would this be? Was it because he was too embarrassed to meet the families and friends of those he had killed? Or was he afraid of the Jewish authorities in Jerusalem, whom he might well have expected to treat him badly as a traitor who had changed sides? He gives us no reason for his absence from Jerusalem and the delay in returning there. We wonder why he did not go back at least briefly to 'clear his desk' and settle up with his landlady.

Gospel for the Gentiles

The only conclusion he wants us to draw is that what had happened to him in Damascus had convinced him that God meant him to preach the gospel to Gentiles. That is what he went to Arabia to do, and then to Damascus and 'the regions of Syria and Cilicia', instead of returning to Jerusalem—except for one fortnight, and that only after three years, when he saw no more than two of the leaders of the church there. He would not build on another's foundations; nor did he need instruction from predecessors. He was doing what he believed he had been called by God to do and he was getting on with it without delay.

It is understandable. If one was suddenly, unexpectedly, and completely convinced that what one had been doing was utterly mistaken and that what one should be doing was the opposite—and that this had been shown to one by God himself—then the most obvious reaction would be to begin the new life immediately, without any delay, and without even returning to apologize and ask for forgiveness.

Paul declared his change of mind by his immediate change of direction—from destroyer of the church to the one who built it up. The churches of Judea recognized what had happened, he says, and praised God for his conversion.

PRAYER

Make us see your will as what we must do, immediately.
Give us a sense of urgency.
May you be glorified because of us.

JAMES *the* LORD'S BROTHER

To some readers of the New Testament, it comes as a surprise to find that there are people mentioned in it who are referred to as 'the brothers (and sisters) of the Lord' (that is, of Jesus). One of them, probably the oldest, is James, whom Paul mentions in this letter (1:19; 2:9, 12) and also in 1 Corinthians 15:7. James is also referred to in Mark (6:3, and perhaps 15:40; 16:1) and Matthew (13:55; 27:56), and the brothers of Jesus in John 7:5, 10; Acts 1:14.

Who were these brothers and sisters? There have been three theories about them. First, that they were the younger children of Joseph and Mary, born after Jesus. Second, that they were cousins of Jesus—the word for brother could cover a wider range of relationships than siblings. Third, that they were half-brothers and half-sisters, being the children of Joseph by a former marriage. The texts in which they are referred to in the New Testament offer us no help at all in choosing between these possibilities.

What Paul says about James in Galatians, and what we read about him in Acts (for example, 12:17; 15:13–21; 21:18–26), is that he became the leader of the church in Jerusalem, and exercised some influence on churches further away—in Antioch, for example (see Galatians 2:11–14), in Corinth perhaps (1 Corinthians 9:5) and in Galatia likewise; this may be why Paul refers to him in this letter.

Much has been written about the extent to which there was a difference in teaching between Paul and James; some have argued for a radical clash of beliefs, while others think that this has been exaggerated.

What cannot be disputed, however, is that Paul refused to accept James, or Cephas, or anyone else, as a standard apostle, or 'pillar', to be regarded as the model for orthodoxy to whom everybody else should conform.

Called by God

In the opening words of this letter, Paul has said that he is an apostle 'sent neither by human commission nor from human authorities, but through Jesus Christ and God the Father, who raised him from the dead' (1:1)—and it is implied that it was God who called Paul from being a persecutor to become his agent without any intermediary between God and Paul. The suggestion, therefore, that what Paul preaches and teaches is different from what James and others in Jerusalem teach and preach, and that Paul is at fault because of this, has no force. Paul is from God, full stop. He is not answerable to anybody else.

To believers who lived in Jerusalem and Judea, and to others who shared their point of view, Paul must have seemed to be a nonconformist, a troublemaker, subversive. At its best, Christianity has always included the right of its members to appeal to conscience against church authority, and to deviate from the opinions, customs and teachings of the majority, even of those in positions of authority. We recognize this in such matters as war, usury, abortion, capital punishment, sexual equality, and in many more areas where people disagree on what is right. In Christianity there is not the same sort of appeal to one authority that we find in Judaism, with the Law of Moses; instead, there is the mind of Christ, the Holy Spirit, tradition, decisions of councils, scripture and so on. This has made for a certain adaptability and variety in Christianity as here in Galatia; Paul is convinced that the practice of the churches in Jerusalem and Judea is not acceptable for Gentiles, and that it is not the business of James (even though he is the Lord's brother) or of Simon (even though he is Cephas, the Rock) to make decisions that affect the churches that he (Paul) has founded.

PRAYER

Thank you for the faith of Paul,
for his courage and independence.
And thank you for the guidance of the Holy Spirit,
both then and now.

PAUL FIGHTS *for* OUR FREEDOM

Paul continues his brief and selective autobiography. His purpose is to demonstrate his independence of all other Christian groups, particularly the church in Jerusalem. His reason for doing this is that people in Galatia are saying that Paul is wrong and that the Jerusalem church is right. They keep the Law of Moses, he does not. Paul's argument is that he is dependent on God for what he says; therefore he must be believed.

He begins now (2:1) to describe his next visit to Jerusalem, the second after his conversion (and, as far as he says in this letter, the only other time that he went there, before writing to the Galatians). In Acts 15 there is an account of a meeting in Jerusalem at which Paul was present. It is probably a different version of the occasion which Paul is describing here, told more from the side of those who disagreed with him. The Acts' account is sometimes described as the Council of Jerusalem and Paul is presented as answering hostile questions to those in authority. Paul's version of the event puts a different light on it. He tells the Galatians what happened in a way that shows that he was answerable to no one except God. The second visit was fourteen years *after*—either after his conversion or after the first visit. He is not, therefore, one who must constantly report back to a higher authority in Jerusalem. He did not go alone; Barnabas and Titus went with him. Both of them will be mentioned further on (vv. 3, 13), and the reason for referring to them may be that Paul wants to show that he alone stood out for the truth of the gospel.

He did not go simply by his own choice, nor was he summoned by the church in Jerusalem to come up and explain himself to them. He went because of a revelation, that is, in response to God. He gives no further explanation of this but his motive is clear. He is not in a position to be called upon by others to give an account of his ministry. Any discussion of his preaching was only at a private meeting—not before a plenary session of the whole church in Jerusalem. He had taken part in this discussion so that what he was doing in his ministry might not be destroyed by others; might not be 'in vain'.

He had in fact been trying to prevent a situation like that which had developed in Galatia, where troublemakers were saying that the

Jerusalem church was the model for all other churches and that the Law of Moses was to be kept by Gentile Christians. The reference to Titus is ambiguous: does Paul mean that it was not required that Titus be circumcised, so he was not; or that he was circumcised, though the Jerusalem church did not require it? Whichever he meant, Paul refers to the subject because others had used it as a case in point. They said that it proved that they were right. Paul denies this.

Paul's purpose, he says, was to maintain freedom for Gentile believers, in the face of false Christians who wanted to bring them into slavery; he was doing this for the sake of his present readers in Galatia (you), that they might be free.

Paul introduces words and ideas that will play an important part in the argument as he sets it out in the rest of this letter. The terms he uses are slavery and freedom, ideas that would be immediately understood in the Roman empire where everybody was either a slave or a free person. Galatians is a plea for Christian liberty. It contains more than a third of all the instances of the word 'freedom' in the New Testament, and more than a quarter of the instances of the adjective 'free'.

What enslaves us in religion is fear of irrational taboos and superstitions; prohibitions create a sense of guilt in those who break them, or who live in terror that they may. The gospel releases those who are threatened by such fears.

Mark, whose Gospel is closest to the insights of Paul, presents Jesus as one who taught that all food was clean and that what defiled was what came from within (from the heart) not anything that entered from without (7:1–23).

Thank God for Paul! He has delivered us from fear of things that we have no reason to fear: the number thirteen; walking under ladders; a single magpie; the predictions of astrologers; things to do with colour, race and sex. Magic was a thriving industry in the first century AD and Christianity was its enemy. In Matthew's Gospel the magicians worshipped Christ—and they handed over the tools of their trade and the money they made by it.

PRAYER

Thank you for the gospel.
Thank you for freedom from fear and superstition.
Thank you for all who have defied the irrational in the name of Christ.

The FREEDOM WE HAVE
in CHRIST JESUS

This letter of Paul's is, as we have already seen (Introduction, page 17), a plea for Christian liberty. The Greek word is translated as 'freedom' in the NRSV (2:4; 5:1, 13); Paul contrasts freedom with slavery, but also with imprisonment (3:23).

He could speak of prison from experience. When he is writing to the Corinthians, he says of those who preach another Jesus and a different gospel, that he has been in prison far more frequently than they (2 Corinthians 11:23). He knew exactly what it was like to wake up in the morning and realize that your freedom to choose what you would do during the day had been drastically reduced. He knew also what it was like to walk out of a prison, breathe the fresh air and feel the sun on your face.

He did not believe that keeping the Law of Moses made you free; it was not the law of liberty (James 2:12). It was because he knew this that he was so determined to fight for freedom in Galatia. He would not have become all things to all people (1 Corinthians 9:22) had he not believed himself to be no longer under the Law.

The workings of the Law

The reason why this was so was that the Law made distinctions: between people (Jews and Gentiles), between different kinds of food (clean and unclean), and between the days of the week (working days and the sabbath). Paul now believes that each of these distinctions is no longer valid. Christ has abolished them, and restored unity in the world; the gospel of Christ breaks down the barriers that the Law had set up.

At the beginning of the world, there had been unity in Adam; Christ, the last Adam, abolishes the divisions that followed the first man's sin. This is why we are free to ignore the old distinctions. God had demonstrated that this was so, because when the gospel was preached, Jews and Gentiles alike received the Spirit and performed miracles. Paul's mission to the Gentiles depended on his realizing what had happened.

He had to oppose those who preached another gospel (1:8, 9); there could be no compromise on this issue: if the food laws were still to be observed, Gentiles would then be compelled to live like Jews, as Peter had demonstrated at Antioch (2:14), and the result of that would be that Christ would have died for nothing (2:21).

The story of the founding of the churches of Galatia would not otherwise have made sense. It was God who gave the Spirit to Gentiles and perfomed miracles among them. Their Christian origins demonstrated the end of the Law. The freedom that God exercised in his dealings with the Galatians (and with people in every other place where the gospel was preached) should be matched by the same freedom in those who believed. They should see themselves as free to love anybody—everybody.

PRAYER

Thank you for your gift of freedom.
Give us the faith to accept it,
and help us to set free those who remain prisoners.

GOSPEL, NOT TRADITION

In Jerusalem, as later in Galatia, Paul was faced with people who had not realized the implications of what they believed. The gospel is the enemy of superstition, the arbitrary and the taboo (which includes much of what was commanded and prohibited in the Law of Moses). It also refuses to be stifled by tradition. What was the case in the past may be so no longer and every appeal to antiquity has to be scrutinized in the light of freedom and universality. Paul is explaining this in these three verses (6–8) and the significance of them is vast.

His account of his second visit to Jerusalem is told in such a way that it will answer a question that was to arise later, in Galatia. People in Galatia will say, 'How can Paul be right and the Jerusalem church leaders wrong over such an important issue as the keeping of the Law of God? How can anyone think that those who were with Jesus in the days of his flesh were mistaken and are still in the dark? Must they not be closer to the truth than a man who did not know Jesus then and who says himself that he had very little contact with them later?'

It is the argument from tradition, against anything that is seen to be an innovation, and it has always had great potency in religious matters. Paul is here rejecting it.

Leadership examined

Who are these 'acknowledged leaders'? He must be referring to Cephas/Peter and to James, among others. Simon had been given the nickname Cephas, 'Rock', by Jesus—but Paul did not draw the conclusion from this that everything Peter did was right. (He will demonstrate this in verses 11–14, below.) James was the Lord's brother—but that relationship did not guarantee his authority, Paul says.

He gives his reason. What they were, in the past, makes no difference to Paul, in the present; because God is no respecter of persons (as the Law itself says in Deuteronomy 10:17). God is not bound by the past. He raised Jesus from the dead (1:1) and he can deliver us from restrictions and limitations, even from matters that are as close to Paul and his readers as the events in the life of Jesus. (Once again, Mark's Gospel illustrates the same idea: 'Who are my mother and my brothers?' 3:33.) God can initiate new beginnings; he has done so, in the case of Paul himself.

The leaders of the Jerusalem church, Paul says, 'contributed nothing' to him. They did not add anything to what Paul had, by then, been preaching for at least fourteen years. They did not insist that he went back to all the churches he had founded and tell them all to keep the Law of Moses. On the contrary, they agreed that God was working through Paul in churches where the Law was not observed, just as he was working through Peter in churches where the Law was being observed.

Ministry and transformation

You could recognize the activity of the same God in both cases. It was the same Jesus who was preached, the same death and resurrection; the same Spirit was received and the same miracles followed. God was not restricted by uniformity. He could be seen as the lover of variety, empowering Peter for a ministry to those who continued to keep the Law, and empowering Paul for a ministry to those who did not.

The extraordinary importance of the letter to the Galatians is that it is evidence for the change within the first generation of a movement that began as a subdivision of Judaism, into something that did not remain within that original setting and culture. The ugly duckling has turned into a swan. It never was a duckling—and now it has grown up it is seen for what it really is.

PRAYER

Give us ears to hear.
Teach us to let go of the past.
Give us courage.

GRACE *to* RECOGNIZE GRACE

Paul's account of his second visit to Jerusalem, and of the meetings that took place at that time, ends with the statement that James, Cephas and John acknowledged that God was at work in Paul. James, the Lord's brother, is mentioned first—perhaps because he had become the overall leader of the church in Jerusalem. Cephas is Peter, and John is one of the sons of Zebedee. (This recognition was similar to what happened in Judea, when the churches there glorified God because of Paul after his first visit to Jerusalem.)

Paul was to go to the Gentiles, and they would go to the Jews. The only request they made of Paul was not that he should teach his converts to keep the Law of Moses but only that Paul and those who were associated with him should 'remember the poor', that is, the believers in Judea and Jerusalem. This was something that Paul was already eager to do. (We know that he fulfilled this instruction because he refers to 'the collection for the saints', in Romans 15:25–29, 1 Corinthians 16:1–4, and 2 Corinthians 8 and 9.)

If, therefore, the troublemakers in Galatia are saying that they have the authority of the church in Jerusalem, either they are lying, or the leaders in Jerusalem have forgotten what was decided, or they have subsequently changed their minds. Paul's argument is that he was doing in Galatia what had been agreed in Jerusalem. Paul was recognized as partner with the Jerusalem leaders. (The word Paul uses is from the same group as the word used of another James and his brother John in Luke 5:10—they 'were partners with Simon' in the fishing industry.) Shaking hands was a symbolic act expressing fellowship, partnership.

Law in transition

If, as many think, this meeting is the same as that described in Acts 15, there are obvious differences between Paul's account of it and Luke's. In the latter, an agreement is reached about what may have been minimum regulations for ritual purity to be expected of the Gentiles. Paul says nothing about this either here or elsewhere. But in any case, what is surprising is that both accounts, Paul's and Luke's, agree that circumcision was not required of Gentile converts.

This is remarkable. What had already been stated as a law for all generations in scripture (Genesis 17) was now no longer accepted as necessary for all members of the people of God, the seed of Abraham. Jesus is believed to be 'the end of the law' (Romans 10:4) in the sense that observance of some laws now ceases to be necessary. The Law-keeping church in Jerusalem had agreed to that. It must have taken some grace to do so.

It takes grace to recognize grace. It takes the Spirit of God to release us from our good and helpful religious traditions when they have become a hindrance to what God is about to do. God is not trapped by the past, but is always dragging his people forward, releasing them from restrictions that may have been useful at one time but have now ceased to serve his purpose. The direction in which he is moving is always towards greater freedom and diversity with less uniformity. Without grace we hang on to the past and reject the liberty that he is offering us.

PRAYER

Release us from what holds us back.
Give us grace to recognize your grace.
Demolish us and rebuild us.

13 GALATIANS 2:11–14

PAUL REBUKES PETER

Paul moves on now from the account of his second visit to Jerusalem to the next incident in his summary of the past. In Antioch (in Syria) an arrangement had been reached whereby the whole church, both those who had been Jews and those who had been Gentiles before their conversion, joined in one common meal. Paul and Barnabas were there when Cephas arrived and at first he joined in this practice of eating with the Gentiles. But he changed his mind when a group of Jewish Christians from Jerusalem arrived—possibly sent by James the Lord's brother in order to make sure that what was happening in Antioch could have the approval of the church in Jerusalem.

Whatever the reason for their coming to Antioch, their arrival and Peter's withdrawal from the common meal caused a crisis in the church in Antioch. It divided into two: Jewish Christians (including Barnabas, Paul's assistant) against the Gentile Christians.

Paul believed that one of the implications of the gospel was that Christ had died for everybody. Everybody had sinned, but now there was one act of righteousness that put everybody, equally, right with God. The distinction between Jews and Gentiles had been abolished (Romans 3:21–31). Therefore, to Paul, what the Jewish Christians were doing was not consistent 'with the truth of the gospel'.

He addressed Cephas, but he spoke to him 'before them all'. Cephas had changed his practice; therefore he was the obvious target for Paul's rebuke. His influence, no doubt, had contributed to the action of the other Jewish Christians in departing from the common meal. But what Cephas had done was in fact worse than that, because Paul assumed (without saying it explicitly) that there can only be one common meal in the church. If there were two—one for ex-Jews and another for ex-Gentiles—neither would be the common meal.

Therefore, if Peter is insisting on the observation of Jewish food laws in the meal, he is now compelling ex-Gentiles to 'live like Jews'. He had formerly lived like a Gentile himself, before the people from Jerusalem arrived; but now he has given that up. What sort of faith in the truth of the gospel is this?

It looks as though the agreement that had been reached in Jerusalem, that Paul described in the previous verses (2:7–10), had been made without anyone foreseeing the problems that would arise in a mixed congregation. Peter could go to Jews, Paul could go to Gentiles, and all would be well if their converts never met. The Jewish believers could continue to keep the Law and the Gentile believers need not. The situation in Antioch provoked an unexpected crisis.

Explosive truth

'The truth of the gospel' is always waiting to burst out on us. It is like a time-bomb that can go off at any moment. When it does go off, it demolishes assumptions and practices that we have adopted without question concerning (for example) class or colour or sex. Peter is reasserting the pre-Christian ideas of Judaism, so he needs Paul to 'oppose him to his face'.

We only have Paul's side of the argument. No doubt there were those who would have said that Paul needed Peter: tradition and the past must not be completely abandoned. Paul would have agreed. He continued to study the scriptures and he did not, like Marcion in the second century, reject the Old Testament as irrelevant to Christianity.

Peter needs Paul to rebuke him and Paul needs Peter to express the need for tradition, continuity, the wisdom of the past, God's revelation of himself in former times. The activity of the church is always an educational process and it requires people with different gifts and personalities to uphold and preserve the necessary traditions. No one person has the whole truth. God works through a variety of gifts and the mutual contradictions and disagreements of individuals. Paul was to say so, later, to the Corinthians: 'There have to be factions [literally: heresies] among you, for only so will it become clear who among you are genuine' (1 Corinthians 11:19).

PRAYER

Teach us to oppose what is inconsistent with the gospel.
Make us willing to be rebuked.
Move us all towards greater understanding of the truth.

NOT *by* WORKS *but by* FAITH

The remaining verses of chapter 2 (15–21) are an elucidation of what Paul had meant when he opposed Cephas in Antioch. When Paul has completed this part of the letter he will immediately deal with the situation in Galatia: 'You foolish Galatians!' (3:1).

What has happened in Galatia is a repetition of what had happened earlier in Antioch. The foolish Galatians are making the same mistake as Peter: they are going back on the freedom they had begun to practise in order to keep customs and regulations that are now out of date. The gospel has made the Law antiquated. To attempt to revive it is to be a renegade.

Paul says that 'we ourselves' (he and Peter and Barnabas and all other Jews who have become believers) have had a change of mind. Previously they used to think that being right with God involved them in keeping the Law as set out in scripture. But now they no longer think that this is so. Instead of keeping the laws, what matters now is Jesus Christ. He has assured them of God's approval of them. This relationship between Jesus Christ and these former Jews, what it is that has changed their minds and the way they live, is called *faith*.

At this point in his letter Paul is setting up with all the clarity that he can muster the contrast between obedience to the Law of Moses (which he calls 'works of the Law' and which includes circumcision, food laws, sabbath observance) and 'faith in Christ' (which excludes obedience to the Law). This is not a contrast between doing something and doing nothing, as though Jews were active and believers were inactive. It is a contrast between two levels of activity. Above all, the Law requires you to separate yourself from those who do not keep it (see 2:12: Peter 'drew back and kept himself separate'). But Christ and faith in him involve no such practices. The way of Christ, Paul will say, is 'through love to become slaves to one another' (5:13). There is no limit to this, but complete freedom: Christ died for all.

How did Paul know that no one will be justified by keeping the Law? He knew it from his experience of keeping the Law, and of being 'far more zealous for the traditions of my ancestors' than many of his contemporaries (1:14). That had led him to persecute the church of God and try to destroy it (1:13). On one side of the contrast were

Law and the destruction of the church; on the other side were faith and being right with God. Works of the Law and faith were therefore mutually exclusive alternatives. You could either keep the Law and be God's enemy (as Paul had been) or you could be a believer in Christ and be right with God.

Peter's reversal

Peter had abandoned the Law (of clean and unclean food) at Antioch, until people came from Jerusalem. Then he had changed his mind. He decided that what he was doing was against God's will and that it was sin. So he had gone back to keeping the Law, taking all the ex-Jews with him except Paul. He was declaring publicly that what he had done in faith (eating with Gentiles) was sinful. He was, therefore, Paul says, making out that Christ, in whom he had believed, had led him into sin. (The NRSV translation: 'a servant of sin' is not as good as the REB translation: a 'promoter of sin'.)

Paul is using the kind of argument called *reductio ad absurdum*; hence his denial of the conclusion: 'Certainly not!' The validity of the argument here depends on the assumption that it was Christ who had led Peter to join the common meal at Antioch in the first place. Peter could reply to Paul that he (Peter) had been mistaken and that Christ had not intended him to do this.

Paul is so convinced of the implication of the gospel and of Christ as the end of the Law that he does not pause to reflect that Peter may not have shared his clarity on this matter. He had attributed Peter's changes of action to *fear*—'fear of the circumcision faction' (2:12). Fear and faith are opposites (see Mark 5:36: 'Do not fear, only believe').

PRAYER

Let us not be afraid of our freedom.
Thank you for our justification.
Thank you for faith.

JUSTIFIED

In 2:16 Paul uses, for the first time in this letter, a Greek word that is translated 'justified' in the NRSV. There is a note in the margin that tells us that the translation of this word could be 'reckoned as righteous'. In Greek, there is no distinction between righteousness and justification.

There is one group of Greek words that all have the same stem or beginning—*dik*. The word means righteous, justified, justify, just, justification, and righteousness. These words come frequently in this letter: fourteen times, in fact, but mainly in the section from 2:15 to 3:21. That is to say, they come in the part where Paul is arguing with the troublemakers in Galatia on the basis of quotations from the Greek translation of the Old Testament.

Paul has to reply to his opponents; they say (quite rightly) that it is clear from scripture that the Law of Moses is to be kept 'throughout your generations'; that is, for ever (Genesis 17:12). Paul's answer to this is that there are two passages in which it is said that righteousness is reckoned, not because of the Law, but because of faith. The first of these is in Genesis 15:6: 'And he [Abraham] believed the Lord, and the Lord reckoned it to him as righteousness.' Paul will quote this passage at 3:6.

The second passage is from the prophet Habakkuk 2:4: 'Look at the proud! Their spirit is not right in them, but the righteous live by their faith.' The NRSV margin says, 'or faithfulness'. Paul quotes this passage in Galatians 3:11: 'The one who is righteous will live by faith' or, as the margin says, 'The one who is righteous through faith will live.'

The Galatians, led on by the troublemakers in Galatia, are beginning to think that, in order to please God and be at peace with him, they should keep the Law of Moses and accept the rules and regulations that would be regarded as essential by the members of the synagogues. This is why Paul will say to them, further on in this letter: 'You... want to be justified by the law' (5:4); that is, through keeping the law.

A faith that saves

Paul believes that this is a mistake that has been imposed on the Galatians by the troublemakers. This is part of the different gospel that he referred to at the beginning of the letter (1:6ff.). The truth of the gospel (2:5, 14; 5:7) is that through the Spirit, by faith, we eagerly wait for the hope of righteousness (5:5). By 'the hope of righteousness' Paul means the assurance we have that God will approve of us at the last judgment, set us on his right hand and welcome us into his kingdom. In the meantime, faith accepts this promise and lives by it, trusting that what we believe will in fact take place.

This is how it comes about that we already live the life of being right with God, through faith in Jesus Christ. There is no need for us to do the things that the law instructs us to do (e.g. circumcision, the food law, the sabbaths and the festivals); to do them would be to turn away from faith in Jesus Christ. Law and faith are, at this point, mutually exclusive; it must be either, or; one or the other; it cannot be both.

PRAYER

Thank you for your acceptance of us.
Thank you for Christ who reconciles us to you.
Keep us in this faith.

HE LOVED ME

As Paul comes to the end of his account of events in the past he returns to the point at which he had begun. He had been a zealous Jew who persecuted the church—until God intervened, revealing his Son to him (1:13–17). God had transferred him from one side to the other. It was like death and resurrection.

'Through the law I died to the law.' Keeping the Law made him condemn Jesus and his followers as blasphemers. But when God revealed who Jesus was, Paul immediately saw the Law as out of date and knew himself to be released from it. So it was God who was the cause of the change in Paul. Therefore, when he 'died to the law', the alternative was to 'live to God'.

The antithesis is very bold, since Jews and troublemakers in Galatia, and the foolish Galatians who believed the troublemakers, would all say that the Law was the Law of God. Paul, on the other hand, is saying that the Law is the opposite of God and that God is the opposite of the Law—and that he had experienced this in his own life.

He then takes up a metaphor to express this change from death to life. Jesus had died by the Roman method of executing slaves—crucifixion. God had raised him to life. Paul, like other New Testament writers, does not say of Jesus, 'He lived and died' but always 'He died and lives' (see, for example, Romans 6:10). The life of Jesus followed his death and began on the day of his resurrection. In the same way, Paul's life (in the real sense) began after his conversion, which was like crucifixion and resurrection. The old came to an end and the new began. (When Paul is writing to the Romans, in chapter 6, he will remind them that their initiation into the church was by baptism and that the meaning of the action was sharing in Christ's death and resurrection to a new life.)

God glorified in Paul

But it is more than a change of circumstances or of manner of life. It is not just that Paul has stopped keeping the Law and adopted a Law-free lifestyle. Paul has died and someone else is now living in Paul. When he said, 'They glorified God because of me' (1:24), the Greek could have been translated, 'They glorified God in me.' God had taken over and Paul was the place in which he was working. Similarly here: 'It is no longer I who live, but it is Christ who lives in me.'

He explains what this means. His present life (in 'the flesh', which will last until Christ returns and flesh and blood are changed into spirit and glory) is lived 'by faith', and faith is union with Christ to such a degree that the actions performed by Paul are really the actions of Christ.

Paul has come to this understanding of himself through his reflection on the gospel and on what God has revealed to him of its meaning. Jesus chose to die: it was an event which he willed to happen. He did it, Paul believes, for the sake of everybody and its effect was universal. One died for all, therefore all were dead. And he did this because he loved all—there could be no other reason. Paul had never known Jesus before the crucifixion. But Jesus knew Paul, and 'loved' him, and 'gave himself' up to death for him.

Unilateral love

It was a one-sided thing to do. That is what *grace* is. It is God being *for* people, Christ dying for people who are sinners, weak, his enemies. The Law, on the other hand, requires obedience. Christ's love and God's are unilateral, entirely independent of the response of those who are loved. To return to keeping the Law, and think that one's status as right with God (i.e. 'justification' or 'righteousness'; it is the same word in Greek) depended on obedience to the Law (as Paul had done before his conversion, as Peter was doing at Antioch after the arrival of the people from James, and as the foolish Galatians are doing now), is to make nothing of 'the grace of God'. It is to reject the offer of a free gift and insist on paying for it.

PRAYER

Make us understand that we are loved.
Overcome our reluctance to receive your gifts.
Stop us from justifying ourselves.

WAS IT *the* LAW *or the* GOSPEL?

Paul has been inviting the Galatians to reflect on what has happened. He began with his life before his conversion and after; then the two visits to Jerusalem; then the incident at Antioch. All through, the argument has been that God works through faith in Christ without the keeping of the Law. But up to this point the events he has referred to have been occasions in which the Galatians themselves were not involved. Now, however, he argues from a fact within their own experience.

There is one thing they cannot possibly deny: they did receive the Spirit. There was a day when something happened, and they all understood it to be the coming of the Spirit into the Christian community in Galatia. Paul does not describe it, because he had no need to: they all knew what he was talking about. It was a day no one could forget, similar to our 'What were you doing when you heard that President Kennedy had been shot or that Margaret Thatcher would not stand for re-election?' It was probably marked by supernatural events—speaking with tongues, prophesying, healings and miracles.

What happened to assure them that they had received the Spirit was not in question: what was to be considered was what they were doing at the time. This is 'the only thing' that they need to reflect upon. Were they doing the works of the Law (circumcising baby boys, keeping the sabbath, observing food laws, as all Jews should) or what were they doing?

Faith comes through hearing

The answer had to be, 'They were listening to Paul as he preached the gospel of the dying and rising Christ.' Faith came through hearing, and what was heard was the good news about the death and resurrection of Jesus.

But notice that Paul says: 'It was *before your eyes* that Jesus Christ was publicly exhibited as crucified'—not, '*in your hearing*'. He will come back to his first visit to Galatia in the next chapter and he will say there that it was because of sickness of some kind that he first preached to them. This was a temptation for them to scorn him. But they did not: they welcomed him as Christ Jesus.

In the world in which Paul lived the expectation would be that the agent of a god would be taken care of by his lord: he would not be sick or accident-prone or experience any sort of failure (4:13–15). But the Galatians did not despise Paul or reject his message: they saw in this sick man the agent of the crucified Saviour, and miraculously they believed and received the Spirit.

How foolish they are, then, to go on now to keep the Law with its regulations. He dismisses these matters as 'flesh' in order to contrast them with the Spirit. By the Spirit God had incorporated the believers into his own life; they were partakers in the existence of God. They could not have more than that. Why ever, then, begin to keep the Law?

Bonanza

The way their Christian life began is the key to understanding how it will go on. It began with something coming out of the blue, without any fulfilment of preconditions. It was sheer grace, gift, bonanza. This sick man stood up and talked, and God took over; that was it. That is how it will be, always: everything depends on God, who is always ahead of his servants, going before them, initiating their good works, pouring his goodness upon them, freely. Not waiting for any response, but making response possible by the gift of faith.

We have the evidence in ourselves. We are his handiwork, the product of his grace. Just as we did not ask to be born, so we did not ask to be born again. We did nothing to qualify. It is all grace. Paul's argument is that if we remember how it is with us we shall understand the ways of God: we can read them off from our own experience.

PRAYER

We did nothing to earn your grace.
While we were enemies, we were reconciled to God.
We received the Spirit without asking.

DESCENDANTS *of* ABRAHAM

The character of Paul's letter changes here. So far it has been mainly autobiographical, but now it becomes expository. Between 3:6
and 5:1 Paul will quote and comment on at least a dozen passages
of scripture. His purpose is to show that he is not being anti-scrip-
tural in not requiring Gentile believers to keep the Law; scripture
itself is on his side. We must suppose that he is answering his opponents, who also will have quoted scripture in support of their con-
tention that Gentile Christians should be circumcised and live as
Jews. They have therefore determined which passages should be
used—and the institution of circumcision at the time of Abraham
was an obvious example. Paul begins his expository section here by
taking up texts from Genesis in which God's dealings with Abraham
were recorded.

As we have seen already (in the Introduction) when it came to
scripture the opponents had the better case. Paul's argument depends more on what has happened recently than on what had happened in the past. That may be why he puts autobiography before
exposition of scripture in the letter. He believes that the real meaning
of the Law is only seen by those who 'turn to the Lord' (2 Corinthians
3:16). Gospel, faith, conversion, baptism and the gift of the Spirit all
come first. Then, after that, the reading of scripture, which will reveal
its truth to those who, through faith, already know what it is they are
looking for.

Who are the descendants of Abraham? This was the question that
the row in Galatia raised. Paul's opponents said it was those who were
circumcised. Paul says it is those who have faith. They could appeal
to Genesis 17; he appeals to an earlier chapter in Genesis, namely
15:6. (The word 'believed' in Greek is the verb that is formed from
the word 'faith': there is no difference in Greek between 'faith' and
'belief'; or between 'having faith' and 'believing'.)

Paul has another passage from Genesis (12:3, also 18:18) to show
that God had foretold the blessing of the non-Jewish nations (i.e. the
Gentiles) in, or by, Abraham. What was it, therefore, that Abraham
had and the Gentiles might have also? Not circumcision and the rest
of the Law; if they adopted that, they would no longer be Gentiles.

Gentiles would be blessed by having faith, in exactly the same way that Abraham had faith.

Understanding the blessing

Paul does not explain at this point in his letter what is meant by 'faith'; he does not describe the content of faith. He will do that later, when he writes to the Romans (chapter 4), perhaps because people had asked him to explain how Abraham's faith could be reproduced in Gentiles now. Both, he says, believe in God who raises the dead: Abraham believed that God could give a son to a couple who were as good as dead; Christians believe that God raised his Son from the dead. But here, in Galatians, he is content to argue by means of words that are not well defined or given any specific content: 'faith', 'righteousness' and 'blessing'. They derive their meaning from the context in which they are used. Who are the descendants of Abraham? Those who have faith; they are the righteous; God's blessing is on them. All this was established in Genesis 12 and 15 before there was any mention of circumcision, and 430 years before the Law was given (see notes on Galatians 3:17).

It is almost inevitable that in any association of men and women somebody will want to define the boundaries of the group. Judaism provided straightforward answers to the question, 'Who is in, who is out?' These answers were, in principle, matters of fact that could be checked and established beyond doubt. Jesus, however, could be quoted as one who rejected this style of thinking: he would not endorse John's attempt to stop a man who exorcized demons using the name of Jesus but who refused to be a member of the group of disciples (Mark 9:38–41). There was a parable (in Matthew 25: 31–46) in which those who are blessed and those who are not are equally surprised when they are given their verdicts at the last judgment.

'Who has faith?' is a notoriously difficult question to answer. Fortunately, we do not need to know. We are not to judge; we must leave that to the only one who can!

PRAYER

Thank you for making us the descendants of Abraham, by faith.
Thank you for the promise of our blessing.
Thank you that this promise is for everybody.

CURSE *or* BLESSING?
LAW *or* FAITH?

In these five verses, Paul quotes four passages from scripture: in verse 10, from Deuteronomy 27:26; in verse 11, from Habakkuk 2:4; in verse 12, from Leviticus 18:5; and in verse 13, from Deuteronomy 21:23. He wants to demonstrate from scripture that being right with God depends on faith, not on keeping the Law of Moses. On the contrary, keeping the Law puts one under God's curse. Christ came to deliver us from this curse, by being crucified for us; his purpose was that we might receive what was promised to Abraham, the blessing of God which is the gift of the Holy Spirit (thus tying this paragraph into the argument about receiving the Spirit, in 3:1–5).

As we have seen already (in the Introduction) the letter to the Galatians is rich in contrasts. Pairs of opposites are lined up against one another. Here, Paul contrasts 'curse' with 'blessing', observing and obeying 'the works of the law' with 'faith'. The mistake of the Galatians, he believes, is to try to join the wrong side. They are turning away from a life of blessing to adopt one that he can only describe as cursed.

It needs to be said that this was not how Judaism appeared to the majority of those who had been brought up as Jews from birth; nor how it appeared to the Galatians who were thinking of living as Jews. The Law was compared to light for those in darkness and water for the thirsty; it was a delight to study it and it rejoiced the heart to keep it. The author of Psalm 119 composed twenty-two eight-line stanzas, acrostics on the Hebrew alphabet, in celebration of the Law. Paul's argument is, therefore, not that the Galatians will be unhappy if they keep the Law but that they will not be within the blessing of God. They may enjoy keeping the regulations of Judaism, but they will no longer be free and they will no longer receive the Spirit. They will, he says, be 'cut off from Christ' (5:4).

Practical questions

Paul's arguments may strike us as excessive, oratorical rather than balanced and carefully nuanced. He is writing to Gentiles and he is dealing with a practical question: should they do what the new teachers in Galatia are telling them to do, or not? If he is not using a sledge-hammer to crack a nut, he is certainly drawing on all his resources of scriptural knowledge to defeat his opponents on their own ground.

To understand Paul's conviction that what he is saying is what God means him to say, we need to understand that the source of his certainty lies in his sense of gratitude to Christ: 'he loved me', and not only that; he 'gave himself for me', to death, to becoming a 'curse for us' by the manner of his execution—'Cursed is everyone who hangs on a tree.'

Paul, the Galatians to whom he writes, and we who read his letter, can see something that had not been at all clear before the crucifixion and resurrection of Jesus. We can see that God does not deal with us on the basis of rules and procedures laid down in books and tradition, some of which must appear (at least to us) as arbitrary and irrational. Instead, God relates to us in ways that are personal: the words that are used are words that describe interpersonal relationships: faith, love, gratitude, goodwill, peace and so on.

PRAYER

Thank you for treating us as adult persons.
Stop us from regressing into infantile attitudes.
Give us the boldness that must accompany faith.

PROMISE, NOT LAW

Paul continues to build up the list of contrasted words in order to persuade the Galatians that if they do what they seem set to do they will be making a serious mistake. He begins with the point that when a will is made it cannot be changed by subsequent events. In Greek, as also in Hebrew, one word could mean both a will and a covenant. What Paul wants to make clear is that the Law was given to Israel only at the time of the exodus from Egypt, 430 years after the patriarchs. (He draws this information from Exodus 12:40: 'The time that the Israelites had lived in Egypt was four hundred and thirty years.')

When God was dealing with the patriarchs he dealt in promises. When he gave Israel the Law through Moses he dealt in commandments that had to be obeyed. The latter cannot abolish the former: wills cannot be altered. Therefore God deals with us through promises, not through the Law.

A difficulty could be raised. If we are arguing about circumcision, then it could be said that it was required of Abraham in Genesis 17. Circumcision was there before the time of Moses. Someone may have pointed this out to Paul, or he may have noticed the difficulty for himself, because when he writes to the Romans he adjusts the argument to take account of it and makes the same point by saying that God made promises to Abraham before Abraham was circumcised (Romans 4:9–12). Faith preceded circumcision. Abraham is the father of all who believe, whether they are circumcised or not.

There is another deduction that Paul makes from the quotation in this paragraph from Genesis 13:15: 'and to your offspring' (literally, 'seed'). It is a singular word and so, he says, it refers 'to one person, Christ'. It might be objected that 'offspring' or 'seed' is a collective noun, referring to a group, and that its being in the singular signifies nothing more than that Abraham's descendants can be classed as one group. No doubt Paul would regard this as a quibble. He saw meaning in the singular word and found it providential. We do not know whether his readers found it so too, but (for what it is worth) he does not (so far as we know) seem to have used the argument again.

The point of real substance in this paragraph is the contrast between promise and Law. Law introduces a condition into an arrangement. The one who gives the law is saying, 'You must do this; and if you do not then the arrangement is dissolved and you have no further claims on me.' A publisher's agreement with an author, for example, states what the author must do: the requirements and conditions. If they are not kept the publisher is released from his side of the arrangement. But promises are promises. They stand—whatever the other party may or may not do. They are unconditional, unilateral and indissoluble.

In the case in point, God was promising to give the land of Canaan to Abraham and to his offspring (Genesis 13:15). There were no 'ifs'—'If you do this, I shall give you the land.' It was an absolute statement of what God would do. Therefore, since God could not contradict himself, he must do it.

Gift of the Spirit

When Paul uses the word 'inheritance' (3:18) he is using the term that was frequently applied to the land of Canaan in scripture (in the Greek translation). But to Paul the meaning of the inheritance is now to be found not in the literal sense but in the metaphorical. It refers, he believes, to the gift of the Spirit and to the life of the age to come, of which the gift of the Spirit is the first instalment. Paul is, in fact, repeating in another way the ideas which he had expressed at the beginning of chapter 3: 'Did you receive the Spirit by doing the works of the law or by believing what you heard?' The Spirit was given to us without our doing anything: it just happened out of the blue.

We can see here why Paul thought that the gospel was good news. It was something for nothing, like treasure found in a field, or an unexpectedly valuable pearl that could be sold for a huge profit (Matthew 13:44–46). God does not hedge his goodness with qualifications: he is sheer generosity.

PRAYER

Thank you for your promise.
Thank you for your bounty.
Thank you for your gifts.

21 GALATIANS 3:19-20

No Turning Back

Paul thinks of the members of the churches he has founded as his children. The gospel was the means by which he caused them to be born and he is both mother and father to them. (He will use the metaphor in this letter at 4:19.) What he is doing now is weaning them off their desire to keep the Law; and the method that he adopts here is to find reasons for the Law that they can see are no longer valid.

'Why then the Law?' is the question anyone hearing the letter might raise at this point. Why did God give it to Israel if it was not to be kept? Nothing in scripture said the Law's validity was only for a time. Circumcision, for example, was said to be for all generations. It was an everlasting covenant (Genesis 17:9-14). It was God's will, and God does not change his mind. This is Paul's problem: how can he persuade the Galatians to do this most unscriptural thing—turn away from their desire (surely, they would say, a good, God-given desire) to obey God's will as it was set out by God in the five books of the Law?

The first thing he says is that the Law 'was added'; it was not part of God's original promise to Abraham. Nothing added later can remove the force of the promise, as he just said (3:15). The inferiority of the Law is manifest in the delay before it was given. Why was it added? 'Because of transgressions.' The meaning may be: to create transgressions. The REB translates it as: 'To make wrongdoing a legal offence.' Without the Law we might do things but not know that they were wrong. Of many things we might say: 'They are natural; we all do them; what is wrong with that?' Jealousy, envy, lust, selfishness, greed and anger are all so common that if no one said they were sinful we might not know. Paul is emphasizing the negative aspect of the Law: it can show you that you are wrong and that you do wrong things.

He says next that the Law was always intended to be temporary: 'until the offspring would come to whom the promise had been made'. He is building on the passage from Genesis that he had referred to (v. 16): 'And to your offspring.' That referred to Christ, he had said. Now he draws the conclusion that, because the promise was to Abraham and Christ, the Law (added later than the promise) ends when the promise is fulfilled. God meant the Law to be temporary;

that is Paul's belief. To keep it is to observe instructions that are out of date. The Law has, if you may put it this way, passed its sell-by date.

There is more to come: 'It was ordained through angels.' Jews believed that there were angels present when God gave the Law to Moses at Sinai; but no Jew had previously said (so far as we know) that the angels ordained, or promulgated, the Law. Scripture had said that it was written by the finger of God, and this left little room for the activity of angels. Paul is therefore going beyond what any rabbi would have said about the Law. Angels were inferior to God, and therefore the mediation of angels in the giving of the Law made it a less perfect expression of God's will than it would have been if the revelation had been direct.

Finally, Paul says, the giving of the Law involved the activity of a 'mediator'—i.e. Moses. This again, he believes, shows the inferiority of the Law to the promise. The fact of the presence of a mediator between God, the angels and Israel, explains why it is that the Law is no longer in force. God acted alone when he made promises. There were too many others involved in the promulgation of the Law, and it suffered from their association with it.

These are extraordinary things for a first-century Jew, who had been a Pharisee, to say about the core of his former beliefs. There is no scripture for him to quote in this paragraph. He depends here not on something that was in scripture, but on what God has done in calling him to be an apostle—and in the conflicts and tensions of Paul's life, in his arguing with apostles in Jerusalem and Antioch, and in protecting his children from the errors of the troublemakers.

We can gauge the force of the impact these events had on Paul by the lengths to which he is going here. He is turning his back on what he had believed to be God's greatest gift and man's dearest joy in order to embrace something else: a different way of relating to God.

Instead of laws, promises. Instead of books, a person. Instead of limits and restrictions, freedom. It was like coming out of prison, coming of age, being given the front door key, opening your own bank account, passing the driving test, getting your first car.

PRAYER

Show us what you have given us.
Let us not revert to childishness.
Push us out of the nest.

RELEASE *from* PRISON

What is the relationship between the Law and God's promises? It is not hostile to them, Paul says. (This seems to be the meaning of the Greek which is translated 'contradict' in the NEB.) The Law no more opposes God's promises than the prison service opposes the liberty of the citizen. It keeps people away from liberty temporarily but it does not threaten it.

Paul speculates that God could have given us a law that would have given us access to freedom and life had he wished to do so; but the fact is, he has not. He has given us a law that acts like a gaoler and keeps us locked up.

One way to think of this is to realize that what the Law of the Jews did was to create divisions between what was commanded and what was prohibited. There were working days and non-working days; clean food and unclean food; Jews and Gentiles; what was appropriate for men and what was appropriate for women. There were also those who kept the Law and those who didn't.

Such divisions are just what sin delights in. They create situations in which all sorts of selfish and destructive tendencies can come into play. 'The scripture has imprisoned all things under the power of sin': it has increased the scope we have for sinning by setting up false aims and intentions.

God brings unity

If the Law divides, then what God does is to unite. He is one, as Paul has just said (3:20), and he brings things into unity with himself so that divisions will be overcome. 'Faith in Jesus Christ' gives us access to a way of living that abolishes the differences in which sin flourishes. This is 'the inheritance' of which Paul has spoken (3:18), the promised land now made available and accessible to believers. Here competition, rivalry, selfishness, strife, hatred and jealousy are overcome.

We can see what Paul was expecting to happen from another letter he wrote, probably soon after this one. Christ would come from heaven and destroy 'every ruler and every authority and power'. He would reign until he had 'put all his enemies under his feet'. Then he would hand over rulership to God the Father, and in this way God would be all in all (1 Corinthians 15:23–28).

The angelic beings (rulers, authorities and powers) that had to be destroyed were responsible for the divisions of the world into nations and classes, and for all mutual opposition and hatred between human groups and individuals. The Law was one of these powers: 'The power of sin is the law' (1 Corinthians 15:56). ' The law came in, with the result that the trespass multiplied' (Romans 5:20). Sin, trespass, law and death must all be abolished before God can be everything to everything, uniting his whole creation to himself in peace and harmony.

PRAYER

Thank you for ending the term of our imprisonment.
Thank you for bringing us into the new world.
Thank you for abolishing all that we feared.

NO MORE DIVISIONS

Paul now introduces a way of thinking about God's dealings with the world which was unusual at that time but which was to have many applications in the future. He sees past history as made up of periods of time in which God acted in different ways.

There was the time when God made promises and people lived by faith—in the age of the patriarchs, Abraham, Isaac and Jacob. There was the time when God gave Israel the Law through Moses. There was the time when the offspring of Abraham—Christ—came: and Christ was the end of the Law and the beginning of a new age of faith. When Paul says here, 'Before faith came' and 'Until faith would be revealed', he is abbreviating a larger expression: 'Before Christ came to begin the era of faith'.

The second period, from Moses to Jesus, was a time of imprisonment and loss of liberty. The Law confined us, and would not allow us to do certain things. It was, Paul says, 'our disciplinarian'. He uses a word that means, literally, 'child-leader' and was used of slaves who took children to school. In Paul's time such people were not held in respect.

God's new age

That is all now over: Christ has come; faith has come; we are living in a new age, and the disciplinarian's time is over. We can see for ourselves that this is so. It is obvious that God no longer recognizes the distinction between Jews and Gentiles, which the Law had created by means of circumcision. Faith is what counts, now; and faith is non-discriminatory, non-exclusive. All sorts of people believe. All sorts of people have received the Spirit—the Gentile Galatians for example.

The NRSV translation here (v. 27), 'As many of you as were baptized', is unfortunate. It might suggest that baptism among Christians took the place that circumcision had had among the Jews and thus provided a new way of dividing people—the baptized and the unbaptized. Paul's intention is to say the opposite: baptism abolishes divisions, it does not create them. Baptism is putting on Christ—being dressed so as to be seen as him. He ate and drank with tax collectors and sinners; he died for everybody, and everybody died when he died. A baptized person cannot distinguish between different classes or divisions in society: distinguishing is abolished.

The most relevant division for the Galatians was that between 'Jews' and the rest of humanity ('Greeks'). The Galatians thought that this was still a valid distinction but Paul does not. 'Slave' and 'free' was also an obvious distinction in a society that depended on slavery for its functioning. In the Christian congregation, however, you could not tell who was which: the Spirit did not observe society's rules. 'Male' and 'female', Paul says, is a third distinction that has been abolished. In their relationship with Christ they are equal; and each of them is an equally important member of the body of Christ. (Paul himself found it difficult to put the second and third of these abolitions into practice—neither slave nor free, male nor female—and so have his successors.)

Christ has done for everybody the one thing that needed to be done: he has died for everyone. Every individual, Jew or Greek, slave or free, male or female, is the person for whom Christ died. One label can be attached to every human being.

PRAYER

Let me make no distinctions.
Let me write no one off.
Let me not give honour to one more than to others.

No Longer Children

Paul makes over again the point he had been arguing in the previous paragraph. (He seems to attribute less intelligence to the foolish Galatians than he will to the Romans when the time comes to write to them.)

To start now to keep the Mosaic Law is to do something that is out of date. The heir of a property, the future owner, is not able to exercise his ownership until he comes of age. Until then he has no more power or control over it than a slave has. He is under the control of others until he inherits.

Similarly, Jews and Gentiles were both dealt with by God through restrictions and limitations. The Jews were controlled by the Law, the Gentiles by spiritual beings—some class of angels, referred to here as 'the elemental spirits of the world'.

But now that Christ has come God is dealing with us as adult, mature, grown-up people. God's Son came as one who was under the Law (he lived as a Jew), and this was not to be as an example for us to follow him (as the troublemakers may have said) but to set us free from the Law.

The NRSV translation has caused disastrous confusion in this passage by attempting to be politically correct and changing 'sons' to 'children' (vv. 5–6) and 'son' to 'child' (v. 7). Paul's point is the complete opposite of what the NRSV says. He means, 'You are no longer children'; you are adult, come of age, you have inherited. 'The date set by the father' has come.

Arguing from the facts

How do we know this? Once again Paul employs the argument from the facts. These Galatian Christians, to whom Paul is writing in Greek, sometimes speak in Aramaic, the language of Jesus and his followers. They say *Abba!* They address God as 'Father!' There was a time when they would not have done so—before Paul came to Galatia. It was Paul, the gospel, Jesus and the Spirit that made the difference. These were the markers that the age of the Law was over and the time of the inheritance had come. They were adults now, not children.

The fact that some of the Galatians wanted to keep the Law, and that Paul had to write this angry letter to dissuade them, shows how attractive a religion that provides plenty of regulations for behaviour can be to some people. They wanted to keep the festivals of the Jews (4:10); they would have followed Peter's example at Antioch and kept food laws (2:11–12); the males in the congregation were thinking of the possibility of circumcision (5:2). Paul thinks this willingness to hand oneself over to the observance of religious practices is a sign of weakness, fear and absence of faith. It is a going back to childish ways, not what God requires of them.

Because something is religious it is not necessarily good. There is such a thing as bad religion. The test (which this passage suggests) is: 'Are we being dealt with as adults?' To do things for which no reasonable case can be made (e.g. circumcision and the food laws), or to try to believe impossible things, is not compatible with God's methods of dealing with us. He deals with humans through a human being. His Spirit enlightens our minds. We are made to think.

PRAYER

Stop me from being unreasonable.
Help me to think.
Inspire my mind.

NOT BACK *into* SLAVERY

The Galatians to whom Paul is writing had been Gentiles; otherwise the question of circumcision would never have arisen. As Gentiles they had worshipped pagan gods which, Paul points out, are not gods at all. He thought of them as some sort of malicious spiritual beings, like fallen angels or demons. Therefore, before Paul preached in Galatia and before the Galatians believed the gospel, they 'did not know God'.

The result of his preaching was the opposite to the situation before he came; instead of not knowing God, they came 'to know God'. Paul says that, but then immediately withdraws it. The truth is not simply the reverse of the previous state of affairs. The change from before to after was not the result of something the Galatians did. It was not a human act that altered the situation. The revelation of God's Son, to Paul (1:16) and to the Galatians (as he will explain in the next paragraph, 4:12–20), was the action of God. Paul therefore withdraws 'you have come to know God', and replaces it with 'to be known by God'. 'How God thinks of us is not only more important, but infinitely more important' than how we think of him (C.S. Lewis, *Screwtape Proposes a Toast,* Fount).

Known by God

'To be known by God' means more than his awareness of us or his having information about us. It involves his attitude towards us, his intention and purpose for us. The whole story of the exodus of the Israelites from Egypt is preceded by the statement, 'God looked upon the Israelites, and God took notice of them' (Exodus 2:25). God's knowledge of the Galatians is the cause of both Paul's mission to Galatia and the faith of the Galatians that followed. It is God's decision to be for us and to rescue us from destruction and to associate himself with us. This is how it was in the exodus and this is how it is with those to whom the gospel is preached.

It makes the Galatians' desire to keep the Law all the more tragic: 'How can you turn back again to the weak and beggarly elemental spirits?'—that is, the 'no gods' that had held them in subjection before faith came. How can you turn to them from the God who turned to you? But this is what they are doing. The trouble-makers have introduced them to the observance of a religious calendar and they have accepted this. Paul thinks it is the thin edge of a wedge: they will become observant Jews in no time.

The whole of Paul's ministry in Galatia will be wasted if this happens. He regards joining the synagogue as on the same level as being a pagan. In both cases freedom was restricted by rules, distinctions were established between what was lawful and what was not, and there was nothing to show that the Spirit was present. It was all superstitions, taboos and irrational traditions.

To us today, this must seem un-ecumenical and hidebound, unappreciative of the deep insights of Judaism, which was the religion of Jesus. Paul saw it differently. He was convinced that the gospel had given him an altogether new insight into God and into how God wanted him to live. God's knowledge of Paul created a new situation for Paul. It involved him in a life of activity that he would never have embarked upon had it not been for God. He was sure that to call God 'Father!' was something new and revolutionary.

PRAYER

Thank you for your knowledge of us.
Do not let what you have done for us be wasted.
Keep us from falling back into slavery.

REMEMBER WHAT HAPPENED

The meaning of the opening sentences of this paragraph is obscure: 'Become as I am, for I also have become as you are.' Literally translated, the Greek says simply, 'Become as I because I also as you.' Paul is about to remind them of his preaching to them in Galatia when they first believed. At that time he had already abandoned the strict keeping of the Law in which he had been brought up. He wants the Galatians to do the same: give up both their pagan past and the Law-keeping future into which the troublemakers are trying to seduce them.

'You have done me no wrong' refers to what happened at the time of his initial visit, as he goes on to say. He is once again recalling facts—facts now that were well within their own experience and can be recalled 'as if it were only yesterday'. The extraordinary thing about that first visit was that the faith of the Galatians happened exactly when it was least expected. It was a miracle.

Paul was a sick man; that was the only reason why he had stopped in Galatia and not gone on more quickly to preach elsewhere. (We do not know what his illness was, and there is no need for us to know.) Sickness, like any other unfortunate circumstance, would be interpreted by the Galatians as evidence that Paul was not sent by God. God's messengers, they would assume, would be protected by the power of their God, and be immune to sickness, accidents, dangers and disasters of every kind. (We know that the Corinthians believed this; that is why Paul refutes it in 2 Corinthians. It would seem extraordinary to any first-century pagan or Jew that God's servants could be strong when they were weak.)

Messenger of God

So the temptation to which the Galatians were exposed by Paul's illness was to write off Paul, and Paul's supposed God, as ineffectual and useless. But they did not; that was what was so extraordinary. The miracle was that they welcomed Paul as an angel (or messenger; it is the same word in Greek) of God. They knew that God had blessed them. ('What has become of the good will you felt?' is literally 'where then is the blessedness?' and expects the answer, 'nowhere'. They have forgotten that God gave them faith. They have forgotten all that he has ever done for them.)

At the time of Paul's first visit to Galatia they had been so deeply aware of their debt to God and to Paul his messenger that they would have given him their eyes—and they could scarcely have given him anything more valuable. But now they think of Paul in a very different way. They have gone over to the side of his opponents and he has become their enemy. He has done this simply by telling them the truth: reminding them of the gospel he had preached, of the faith God had given them, of the Spirit they had received, and of the miracles God had performed.

From persecutor to apostle

Paul's way of dealing with the Galatian problem may seem to us rabbinical and quaint: the quotation of texts, often out of context; allegorical interpretations of scripture, and so on. But in fact he is never far from rubbing their noses in indisputable happenings. His life really had changed—from persecutor to apostle. The churches in Judea really had known this—and confirmed it. The Galatians really had received the Spirit through faith—and not through keeping the Law. Paul really had been a sick man, no advertisement for a God to be believed in by first-century pagans. All they had been given to see was a crucified Christ present in his sick apostle—but they really had been blessed with faith.

Telling the truth can make you an enemy of those to whom you do it. Jesus said, 'The truth will make you free'; but they put him to death for saying it.

PRAYER

We fear the truth and resist it.
We do not want to remember your goodness.
Forgive our perversity.

PAUL *is* THEIR FATHER
& THEIR MOTHER

Paul was not writing this letter to us. He was not writing it for anyone other than the Christian congregations in Galatia in the middle of the first century AD. He could assume that they knew things about which we are largely ignorant. When he says, 'They make much of you', he is, it seems, referring to the troublemakers in Galatia—and his readers knew exactly what he meant and what they were doing.

His opponents were zealous in the attention they paid to the congregations, but Paul says that it is not genuine love. Their motives are false. Paul's opponents are telling the Galatians that they are not proper members of Abraham's family, so that the Galatians will ask them to show them what they must do. (The answer they will receive will be, 'Keep the Law, just as all Abraham's genuine children do.') Genuine love is good, but they will not get this from the troublemakers. The only one who really loves them is Paul—and, he implies, no one else.

He was the first to preach the gospel in Galatia. That gave him a relationship with them that no one else could have. He describes this relationship, in another letter, as begetting, fathering: 'For though you might have ten thousand guardians in Christ, you do not have many fathers. Indeed, in Christ Jesus I became your father through the gospel' (1 Corinthians 4:15). In this metaphorical sense he calls them 'my little children'.

But then he switches the metaphor: he is their mother, in the process of 'childbirth' all over 'again until Christ is formed' in them. He has both the responsibility of the father for starting the family and the pain of the mother in bringing them to birth. It does not matter if the metaphor is mixed. All that matters is that he tells them of his love for them and of the pain that they are causing him—and that he uses the fact that they are his converts to drive a wedge between them and the troublemakers.

Paul's ambition

Paul tells the Romans that he made it his ambition to proclaim the good news, not where Christ had already been named, so that he did not build on someone else's foundation (Romans 15:20). He says this with the implied criticism of those who do not keep such a rule; they poach his converts, but he never does that to them.

If we are right in thinking that his opponents in Galatia are part of a larger movement, centred in Jerusalem, which we also meet in Paul's letters to the Romans, the Corinthians and the Philippians, then we can see that they seem to have adopted a policy of travelling round behind Paul, making up the deficiencies in his ministry (as they believed). Paul's irritation and anger are understandable.

To us, Paul may seem over-possessive. We might say, 'It does not matter if they want to do things that I personally do not approve of. And if they find other preachers more helpful than I, let them listen to them. It is all one God, one Christ, one Holy Spirit, whoever preaches and teaches.'

Paul certainly did not take this view of the matter. He did not think that it was unimportant what you believed, or that it did not matter what religious practices you observed. He took the matter very seriously: 'Listen! I, Paul, am telling you that if you let yourselves be circumcised, Christ will be of no benefit to you' (5:2). Their salvation hung in the balance. He must stop them from making a mistake that would cost them their eternal life.

PRAYER

Give us genuine love for one another.
Make us care for others.
Help us to be serious.

The TWO BRANCHES of ABRAHAM'S FAMILY

Paul now uses the scriptural account of Abraham's descendants to demonstrate to his readers in Galatia that, according to the Law itself, it would be wrong for them to keep the Law. It seems highly likely that his opponents were saying: 'Unless you are circumcised you are not part of Abraham's family, that is, the people of God.' Paul is replying: 'By reading Genesis in a certain way we can see that freedom from the Law was foretold in the Law.' It is Paul's final argument against his opponents, and to them (though not perhaps to us) it may have seemed devastating, destroying their whole case.

We have seen already that in this letter Paul is forcing the issue into a choice between alternatives and that he defines the alternatives by means of opposites. He is saying: 'Here is one way, and there is only one other way; choose which you will go along. One is Spirit; the other, flesh. One is gospel; the other, Law. One is blessing; the other, curse.' He now finds these alternatives in the patriarchal legends, symbolized by Abraham's two sons.

The names of the two sons are Ishmael and Isaac. Ishmael, who was born before Isaac, was the son of Abraham by Hagar, the slave of Sarah, Abraham's wife; Isaac was the son of Sarah, conceived when both she and Abraham were of great age. (The name Isaac means 'he laughs': see Genesis 17:19 and 18:9–15.) There was nothing in any way remarkable about the conception and birth of Ishmael; it happened just like any other birth; Paul says it was 'according to the flesh' (v. 23). Isaac's birth was totally unexpected, because of the age of his parents (Paul will make this point more explicitly in Romans 4:19) and Sarah's record of infertility. Isaac was therefore 'born through the promise'. God had said it would happen, and that was why it did happen (Genesis 17:15–22). Each son is the ancestor of a nation: Ishmael of the Arabs and Isaac of the Hebrews.

Re-reading the story

Paul, however, interprets the two branches of Abraham's family allegorically, taking as his key to this exposition the status of the two mothers (Sarah was a *free woman*, Hagar was a *slave woman*) and bringing in also the contrast between *the promise* and *the flesh*. In this way Sarah and Isaac are the symbols of those who believe in Christ while Hagar and Ishmael are the symbols of those who do not. Thus freedom (from the Law) is the mark of believers, slavery to the Law is the mark of unbelievers.

Paul also contrasts Mount Sinai and Jerusalem with the Jerusalem in heaven; the former are associated with Law and the latter with freedom. Finally, he brings in a quotation from Isaiah (54:1) where a childless person (here he means Sarah) is promised more children than a married woman (i.e. Hagar): believers will outnumber unbelievers.

Paul did not find this interpretation of the two women and their sons in scripture: he read it in, rather than reading it out. He read scripture in the light of his Christian experience. And the lesson he learned here was that Abraham's family are not to keep the Law, because they are free. The Law tells us not to keep the Law. It is a *tour de force*.

PRAYER

Show us the extent of our freedom.
Help us to believe in the Spirit.
Thank you for the church, our mother.

CHRISTIAN LIBERTY

Paul now applies the allegory to the situation in Galatia. Those who believe in Christ are 'children of the promise, like Isaac'. He does not mean anything similar to our expression 'promising children'—people with talent, high IQs, future leaders, etc. 'Children of the promise' means people who have come into existence through a special act of God and not in the usual, normal way. They are exceptions because they are believers: and faith requires a gift from God—the gift of being a believer.

The background to the expression, which is essential for understanding its meaning, is Genesis 17:15ff.: God's promise was the cause of Sarah's conception. God's gift of faith was the cause of the Galatians' believing. (We are to remember that they had every reason not to believe Paul, but to 'scorn' and 'despise' him, 4:14.)

Paul then quotes Genesis again: this time it is Genesis 21:10, in which Abraham was told by Sarah to expel Hagar and Ishmael; the inheritance was not to be shared between the slave-branch and the free-branch of the family. Jews persecute the followers of Christ now, Paul is saying, just as Ishmael persecuted Isaac then. The future for the family of Abraham lay with Isaac—those who were free—and that is how it is now. Therefore, do not attempt to join the wrong side.

'Christ has set us free' by his death and resurrection. He has died the kind of death that the Law declared to be cursed (3:13). He accepted the position of being condemned and executed, and the result is that the whole system of Jewish Law under which he was judged has been brought to an end.

Notice once more the word 'again' in 5:1. The 'yoke of slavery' is the Law of Moses, but the people Paul is writing to had been Gentiles before they believed. To be circumcised now, and to keep the Law, will be to go back 'again' to where they were before they believed. There is no distinction in this respect between Judaism and paganism; both are described here as 'slavery'.

A new kind of living

Paul recognizes coming into faith as a kind of living that is new, different, and totally strange. He will list some of the aspects of it in the next chapter, but notice in particular *joy* and *peace*. Anyone who has experienced these knows that they are extraordinary and unbelievable—so extraordinary and unbelievable that they could easily be dismissed and lost in a return to everyday normal existence. Paul will say, in another letter, that 'the peace of God surpasses all understanding' (Philippians 4:7). Our hold on it is tenuous; we must 'stand firm' and not let troublemakers try to convince us that we do not have it.

The irony was that it was religious troublemakers who were causing the trouble and causing one sort of religion to destroy another.

PRAYER

Thank you for freedom, joy and peace.
Help us to resist pressure to doubt it.
No submission to fear!

EITHER–OR

Paul believes that it is not a matter of indifference whether the Galatians keep the Law, or whether they do not. Nor is it possible to pick and choose. It is either–or, and it is all or nothing.

It is either–or, as he has argued all the way through the letter. The two ways are alternatives: you cannot go in two directions at the same time. There is salvation through Christ on the one hand, and there is circumcision and the other laws on the other hand. The Galatians must choose. There had been a before and after in the life of Paul: persecution before, proclamation after. No compromise was possible: 'If you let yourselves be circumcised, Christ will be of no benefit to you.'

It is also all or nothing. Circumcision introduces them to a life of obedience to the Law, and this may involve more than they had expected: its detailed instructions covered the whole of life. Paul then says it again: Christ and the Law are incompatible as ways of salvation.

Paul says nothing about the historical reasons for the crucifixion, or on what charge Jesus was condemned, or even whether he was condemned by a Jewish court. He may not have known. What he did know was that he had thought that the followers of Jesus should be eliminated and he had sought to do so. In his own experience, Christ and the Law had been opposites—enemies, mutually exclusive—and this had ended in the crucifixion of Jesus and the conflict between the authorities of Judaism and the early church.

Troublemakers?

Perhaps there was another element too. Those who kept the Law within the church at Jerusalem may have been (or been thought to be) the instigators of the trouble in Galatia and indeed wherever Paul had established any congregations. The conflict was a daily problem, and he could not dismiss it as of no importance. He refers to it as danger from false brothers and sisters (2 Corinthians 11:26).

Paul will now move on from this subject to another and the rest of the letter will be dominated by two main ideas. First, we do not need the Law because we are led by the Spirit. Secondly, we do not need the Law because there is one commandment that sums it all up: *You shall love your neighbour as yourself.*

We live in a transition period, praying for the end of this age to come quickly. That is the righteousness we are looking forward to, when God will declare us his sons and daughters (Matthew 5:9). Distinctions made by the Law (Jew and Gentile, etc.) are now matters of the past. The evidence is there in the congregations: they are meetings of believers, and they are held together by love: 'The only thing that counts is faith working through love.'

PRAYER

Thank you for the simplicity of the gospel.
Thank you for the abolition of false religion.
Thank you for the clarity of the alternatives.

The OFFENCE *of the* CROSS

The Galatians have changed course since they began to believe. Something had happened in Paul's absence that had made them adopt new ideas to which Paul violently objects. We know only from what we can gather from Paul's letter who it was and what was said, and this is not much.

Paul uses a metaphor from the games (as he does again in 1 Corinthians 9:24–27). They were 'running well', but someone interfered with them (the literal meaning of the Greek word would be 'cut in') and stopped them from 'obeying the truth', that is, the gospel as he had preached it to them. They knew what he was talking about, and he does not go on to identify the intruder. What he does say is that this influence had not come from God (i.e. the one who had called them to believe; see 1:6). It must, therefore, be of the devil; there was no third possibility in a situation such as this. He then switches to another metaphor, this time bread-making. You do not need much 'yeast' to 'leaven the whole batch' (compare Matthew 13:33 and 1 Corinthians 5:6ff. where leaven is used to refer to something evil that must be removed: incest in 1 Corinthians, false teaching in Galatians).

Paul believes that the Galatians will do what he is telling them to do. We do not know exactly what happened next, but it may be that the preservation of the letter points to their having taken his advice and rejected the troublemakers.

Dispute

'Whoever it is that is confusing you' (compare 1:7, 'there are some who are confusing you'; there it is in the plural, 'some'; here it is in the singular, 'whoever') 'will pay the penalty' or, as in the REB, 'must bear God's judgment'. Does the 'whoever it is' mean 'whatever his position and status'? Even if he is the leader of the church in Jerusalem? Even if he is the Lord's brother?

Then, once again, the argument from observable facts is brought in. It cannot be, as some say, that Paul still preaches circumcision. If he were, he would not be being persecuted by Jews or by Jewish

Christians. The undeniable fact that people are against Paul shows that he is still saying things that make them angry with him.

What he preaches is 'the cross': that Jesus, God's Son, was put to death by crucifixion, and that this was according to the scriptures and for our sins (1 Corinthians 15:3). Christ has taken the place of the Law. Those who have received the Spirit are those who believe in him, not those who keep the Law. The saving moment is identified as an act of suffering and shame. This is why Paul speaks of it as an 'offence' (the word is *skandalon*), something that causes you to trip and fall over. This is what the gospel is to Jews; they 'demand signs' (i.e. miracles) but to be crucified is no miracle at all (1 Corinthians 1:22–25).

The anger of Paul with those who are causing trouble in Galatia is evident in the next verse, which one commentator describes as 'downright rude and even objectionable' (Ziesler, *The Epistle to the Galatians,* Epworth Press).

PRAYER

Let us not forget how offensive faith is.
Let us not be surprised that people find it so, and find us so.
Help me to believe that truth will prevail.

GOOD NEWS & OFFENCE

The crucifixion of Jesus is both good news and an offence—that is, something that causes us to reject it. Paul preached it, and he knew from experience that some of those who heard him welcomed what he said and allowed it to change their lives; while others reacted to his preaching in exactly the opposite way: they hated it and they persecuted him for saying it. He refers to these diverse reactions to the gospel in another letter: 'We are the aroma of Christ to God among those who are being saved and among those who are perishing: to the one a fragrance from death to death, to the other a fragrance from life to life' (2 Corinthians 2:15, 16).

How can the one gospel produce such contradictory effects?

If you believed what was being preached, you had the answer to the most perplexing problem that you could ever have to consider: What is the purpose of my existence (if there is one), and how can I achieve it? The crucifixion of Jesus was proclaimed as the message of God's love for his creation and as the means whereby you could enter into a permanent relationship with him, which was the purpose of your existence. The sort of words that Paul used to refer to this were 'justified', 'reconciled', 'glorified' and so on.

This was obviously good news, but what was not good news was the method by which God had acted in order to make this possible. Jesus had been handed over to destruction; he had been put to death in the most cruel and shameful way, with maximum humiliation. But this was said to be in accordance with the scriptures (1 Corinthians 15:3, 4); that is to say, it was thought to be God's will.

Suffering like Jesus

The followers of Jesus and, above all, his representatives such as Paul himself were being treated in the same way: the hatred that Jesus aroused and that led to his crucifixion was now being vented on them. This was no surprise, because, if salvation came through destruction in the case of Jesus, then it would come through destruction for his followers also. But that was to offer them what nobody wants. The usual reaction to humiliation, failure, being taken to pieces, loss and death is violent rejection. This was why

Paul encountered such contradictory effects as the result of his preaching.

What the preacher had to offer his hearers was both a free gift, and something that was more expensive than anything else could ever be. The only way in which you could accept the gift (justification, reconciliation, acceptance by God) was by giving up your life; but without your life, you could not have anything. The dead have no possessions.

If you believed the preacher of the gospel, you were baptized, and this demonstrated the two aspects of the gospel perfectly. In baptism you were united with Jesus in his death (by getting into the water) and in his resurrection (by coming out of the water). You died and you rose. That was how it would be for the rest of your time, until the end: dying and rising. The dying would be the offence, and the rising would be the good news. The demand of God would be total, and so would his gift. He would require your life, and he would give you his.

PRAYER

Help us to hear what you want, and what you give.
Forgive the poverty of our giving.
Open our hearts to your generosity.

ONLY ONE COMMANDMENT

A new section of the letter begins at this point and continues to 6:10. The theme now is *love* and *Spirit*. It may be that Paul's opponents were saying, 'If we do not retain the Law of Moses there will be nothing to prevent us from falling into anarchy. We need the Law to stop us from following our own unbridled selfishness.' It may be that; or it may be that Paul anticipated such an argument. Whichever it was, he now takes up the subject, showing that there are other resources available: *love*, and God's *Spirit*.

'You were called', by God. Paul has used the word three times already in this letter (1:6, 15; 5:8) and in each case of God calling people to believe. The fact of their believing is due entirely to God, not to themselves. He chose them, predestined them, sent Paul to preach to them, gave them the Spirit. Their faith is not of their own doing, but of God's; so who are they to change the terms which were laid down from the beginning? These terms didn't include keeping the Law.

On the contrary, they were invited by God to be free—both from the fears and restraints imposed by their pagan religion and from any other kinds of limitation (such as the Law of Moses). Paul has already contrasted Law and freedom (e.g. in 4:21—5:1, the allegory of the two women, one free and the other a slave). By 'freedom', here, therefore, he means exemption from the Law which imposed prohibitions on its observers.

Misunderstanding freedom

Nevertheless, freedom does not mean freedom to sin. Nor does it mean that if we were free we would have nothing to keep us from sinning. It would be a misunderstanding of freedom, and a misuse of it, to treat it as a bridgehead from which self-indulgence could advance. (The word which Paul uses, *sarx*, translated 'the flesh', is an expression that refers to all kinds of self-centredness and not only what are sometimes called 'sins of the flesh'.)

Paul is not afraid of paradoxes. He knows that the gospel can only be expressed by using them: glory/shame; power/weakness; wisdom/foolishness; and so on. He produces them now to explain what the new life is: to be free is to be the slave of others; this is the effect of love (Greek: *agape*): Christ's love made him our slave, dying for us; our love for one another makes us the slaves of each other.

This is, after all, what the Law itself commanded (Leviticus 19:18): 'You shall love your neighbour as yourself'; and that one commandment sums up all that God intends us to do and all that the Law was intended to achieve. Of course God does not mean us to use our freedom in a destructive way; but we only need one controlling aim to keep us from that.

We shall have more scope for love if we detach it from the Law of Moses. As long as it is part of Moses' Law it may have to be qualified: 'Who is my neighbour?' (Luke 10:29) But taken without any possible restrictions (that neighbour means fellow Israelite, etc.), love can be exercised without discrimination: it was while we were his enemies that 'we were reconciled to God through the death of his Son' (Romans 5:10).

PRAYER

Thank you for our calling.
Thank you for our freedom.
Teach us to fulfil your only commandment.

The HARD ROAD

Paul is not starry-eyed about the Christian life and he does not want his readers to dismiss him as impractical. He knows how members of Christian communities can 'bite and devour' one another; he had a long-running case in Corinth which was probably still on at the time of the writing of Galatians.

The Galatians had received the Spirit (3:2); there could be no denying that. But to have received the Spirit was not the end of the problem. They must still be exhorted to 'live by the Spirit'. The word that Paul uses literally means 'walk'. God's commandments are a way, or road, or path. To obey them is to walk or run in his way. To disobey the commandments of God is to step off his path, to trespass.

The believer is aware of two things, not of only one, in this respect. There is both the power and insight given by the Spirit, but there are also 'the desires of the flesh'. He means, as we have seen, self-centredness and its accompanying destructiveness of others. Or to put it more bluntly: we can either love one another, or not; but if we do not love one another, we shall destroy one another.

We are thus prevented from doing what we want: we are the scene of conflict and warfare: *Spirit* against *flesh* and *flesh* against *Spirit*.

Choosing the Spirit

What we must do is choose *Spirit*, and say no to *flesh*. There is one who will lead us: a guide who will come with us along the road. It is the Spirit; you can be *led by the Spirit*.

Talk of two ways, of walking and trespassing, is all found in the scriptures we call the Old Testament. But there, it is the Law that provides the way of God's commandments and is the light to our path. Now, however, the Law is no longer our guide: 'If you are led by the Spirit, you are not subject to the law.' It is the same pair of opposites that we have had earlier in the letter (e.g. 3:2).

Paul knew what it was to be led by the Spirit. It involved a complete turn-about in his life and endless travel, not always pleasant because of the conditions both on land and at sea (2 Corinthians 11:23–29). But wherever he went, he carried with him a personality that was no light burden. He describes himself, in another letter, as a 'wretched man', in need of rescue 'from his body of death' (Romans 7:24); and in another as having 'a thorn... in the flesh, a messenger of Satan to torment me' (2 Corinthians 12:7).

The warfare between flesh and Spirit was unceasing inside Paul. He had to choose to walk by the Spirit, guided, enlightened, aided and helped. Paul was not pretending that life would be easier if they were led by the Spirit than if they were under the Law. It would be more difficult. It was a narrow road, hard to travel along.

PRAYER

Help us to endure self-despair.
Help us to resist self.
Help us to follow the Spirit.

On the ROAD to DESTRUCTION

There are two roads: one leads to life and the other to destruction. Paul is exhorting the Galatians to follow the one and avoid the other. He thinks there is no problem in distinguishing them; certainly the results of self-indulgence are obvious. Nevertheless, he gives them a list, to make quite sure that they have got the point.

Though the list begins with 'fornication' and includes 'drunkenness' and 'carousing' it is not limited to sensuality. There are 'religious' sins and social sins also, and in fact there is more concerning the problems of living close to other people, as members of the same body, than about individual acts of wickedness.

The question is: Are we to think of ourselves as moving towards our fulfilment in isolation from other people; even in competition with them? Or are we to think of ourselves as members of an association of people, with obligations to them? In later letters, Paul will use the language of *body* and *organs and limbs*. He did not believe that Christianity was to do with what we do with our solitude.

Baptized into fellowship

Paul was not a individualist. He believed that we were baptized into membership of a group, that Christ was the head of a new humanity, a second Adam; and that the sins we commit against the members of the fellowship are incompatible with its purpose: 'enmities, strife, jealousy, anger, quarrels, dissensions, factions, envy'.

In contrast with the list of 'the fruit of the Spirit' in the next paragraph, this list ends with the words 'and things like these'. It lacks both shape and conclusion. It is an ugly list of ugly things we do— *works* contrasted with *fruit* (i.e. what the Spirit produces in us).

The hard road leads to *the kingdom of God*; the other, to destruction. 'The kingdom of God' (an expression Paul uses infrequently in his letters: it comes more often in the first three Gospels) means the time when God will reign—after the Lord has come from heaven and abolished all other rulers, human and angelic (1 Corinthians 15:24–28). Paul does not say, 'Sin is of no importance; we shall be saved by faith, therefore it does not matter what we do.' He believes in a future judgment: 'we will all stand before the judgment seat of

God' (Romans 14:10). He believes that our present relationship with God (our *justification*) depends on Christ and is known by faith; but our situation on the last day will be according to our deeds (Romans 2:6).

PRAYER

Make us understand that we belong with others.
Let us not sin against them.
Show us how much we need them.

The KINGDOM *of* GOD

In each of the three letters that are discussed in this volume (Galatians and the two to the Thessalonians) Paul mentions the kingdom of God once: Galatians 5:21; 1 Thessalonians 2:12; 2 Thessalonians 1:5. In each of these three passages, he is referring to a time in the future, the new age that is to come. The kingdom of God, in these letters, means the day of the Lord (2 Thessalonians 2:2), the time of salvation and glory.

It is very obvious to any reader of Paul's letters that this subject was far more prominent in his time and in the churches he founded than it is in most churches today. Paul had said, at the beginning of Galatians, that Christ gave himself for our sins, to set us free from the present evil age (1:4). Believers understood themselves as those who accepted the crucifixion of Jesus as God's means of delivering them from the age in which Satan ruled, in order that, when the time came, they might enter into the age in which God would rule, that is, God's kingdom.

Calling for God's kingdom

We do not know whether Paul knew the Lord's Prayer. The only New Testament writers who have it are Matthew (6:9–13) and Luke (11:2–4). There may be allusions to it elsewhere in the New Testament, but whether Paul knew it or not, we know that he and the congregation of Corinth knew an Aramaic prayer: *Marana tha*—'Our Lord, Come!' (1 Corinthians 16:22). They prayed for him to come, in order that he might abolish all evil powers and thus enable God to rule in their place: 'Then comes the end, when he hands over the kingdom to God the Father, after he has destroyed every ruler and every authority and power' (1 Corinthians 15:24).

The version of the prayer in Matthew begins with three petitions for this to happen, and in each petition the words are arranged in the same order in Greek: 'Be hallowed your name; come, your kingdom; be done, your will.' This is asked for in such a way that both in heaven and on earth God will make everything new. It is as if we said, 'Finish then thy new creation.' The rest of the prayer consists of four petitions for us to be allowed to join in the feast, having been forgiven in the judgment and having been delivered from Satan and his final great temptation of the last days.

To have this hope and to pray this prayer commits you to a particular way of living. That is the point that Paul is making here in Galatians. The list that he has just given of acts that belong to our 'unspiritual nature' describes the sort of behaviour that is incompatible with the longing for the kingdom to come and asking that it may happen soon. Anyone would be indulging in self-contradiction who said the Lord's Prayer and behaved in the way that the list implies. This was why Paul had warned the Galatians not to do these things, and why he warns them again, now.

PRAYER

Give us purity of heart.
Make us simple, straightforward,
focused on God.

On the WAY *to* SALVATION

'The works of the flesh' came in a list that had no unity or overriding shape. It even had no ending: you could add further actions for yourself, if you wished. Evil is destructive and has no cohesion in itself. But what *the Spirit* produces is very different from that. Paul uses a single word to refer to it: *fruit*. It has unity and shape: the list consists of three threes, and there is no *etcetera* at the end.

Love (Greek *agape*) had to come first, after 5:14: it is the one commandment of God, and all the other aspects of the fruit are further descriptions of love and consequences of it. Notice that *joy* comes second: none of the hardships of the Christian life, to which he referred briefly in verses 16 and 17, in any way takes away from joy. He will say elsewhere that the believer is 'always rejoicing' (2 Corinthians 6:10). *Peace* means both peace with God, and (as much as it is possible) with everybody.

The second group of three consists of longer words in Greek, dividing the nine elements into three plus three plus three. *Patience* is willingness to endure irritation; *kindness* is willingness to seek the good of others; and *goodness* is having aims and plans for others, and seeking their welfare.

The third section returns to shorter words: *faithfulness* here is in Greek the word 'faith' that we have heard all through the letter. But perhaps it refers more at this point to faith between believers, rather than between believer and God. *Gentleness* is willingness to be put upon by others; elsewhere it is sometimes translated 'meekness'. It is not a popular characteristic today; it is the opposite of 'thrusting', 'go-getting', etc. *Self-control* is necessary because 'the desires of the flesh' are still at work in the believer.

Essentials for living together

The nine items on the list are exactly those that one would look for if one were choosing people to be involved in any corporate exercise. They are the essentials for living together and working together; they are what is needed if an association is to be built up and not broken down.

'No law' deals with these matters; they cannot be included in commandments, except for the first, love. They are the opposite of the destructiveness of the flesh (self-centredness). They are the result of God's Spirit, who brings unity out of people who would otherwise be divisive, and creates fellowship among those who might seek their own advantage.

We all agree that the Spirit is the life of the church. Therefore we must be in line with the Spirit, seeking unity with others, allowing the Spirit to produce his fruit in us. The opposite would be conceit, competition, envy.

There is no doubt that Paul understood the meaning of fellowship, community, living together, being part of a society. He stresses it here, at the end of his letter. The troublemakers have divided the churches: he must heal the divisions that they have made—or rather, the Spirit must re-create the fellowship of the Holy Spirit.

PRAYER

Create the ninefold fruit in us.
Destroy our selfishness.
Bring us into unity.

LOVE *in the* CHURCH

Here, as in his other letters, Paul turns finally to practical matters. How is the love which is the one commandment to be worked out in practice?

First of all, there are still faults within the community: the NRSV translation 'transgression' is unfortunate, since this might be taken to imply that Paul believed in the Law. He uses a different word here from that in 3:19 and it means, literally, 'false step'. He had referred, at the end of the previous paragraph, to conceit, competition and envy. The community is not yet perfect.

The rest of the congregation (if that is what he means by 'you'), filled with God's Spirit, are to restore the one who has erred 'in a spirit of gentleness' (the same word as in 5:23). Such action will tempt them to feelings of superiority and conceit and competition: they are to take care that they resist such temptations. They are to remember that they, too, may fall. One way to do this is to enter into the problems of others and feel the tensions they are subjected to. This is 'to bear one another's burdens', and this is the law that Christ both taught (e.g. Mark 12:31) and fulfilled by dying for us.

To think oneself something is to assume a status and position before God from which one can look down on others, as the Pharisee does in the parable (Luke 18:9–14). But this is to forget that our standing before God is entirely through faith in God and Christ. In ourselves, we are nothing. It is remarkably easy for us to deceive ourselves, and take what God has done for us and make it into a reason for looking down on others.

The work of God within us

What we have is the fruit of the Spirit (5:22); our own work is the work of God within us. If we recognize that, we shall see how far short it falls of the perfection that it might be. Self-knowledge is the best defence against arrogance and conceit. The load that each of us has to carry is awareness of resistance to the Spirit and failure to be guided by the Spirit.

The apparent contradiction between the command, 'Bear one another's burdens' (v. 2) and, 'All must carry their own loads' (v. 5) calls for some explanation. It is those who know their own problems who will be best at understanding the problems of others; while the reverse is also the case: it is those who are most unaware of their own problems who will be least sympathetic with others.

Paul may have expected the arrival of his letter in Galatia to have promoted reconciliation in the congregations to which it was to be read—some people accusing others of disloyalty to Paul or of lack of insight and faith. He wants to heal the divisions and restore peace to the communities. His letter has been very outspoken, and the situation will now need careful and loving attention.

PRAYER

Help me to put others before myself.
Give me knowledge of myself.
Remind me that I am 'nothing'.

YOU CANNOT FOOL GOD

So far in the letter there has been no reference at all to the ministry in the churches to which Paul is writing; he has addressed the congregations, not their leaders. But now, in 6:6, we have the one and only mention in Galatians of any kind of minister—a 'teacher'. One of the few references to the words of the Lord in Paul's extant letters is in 1 Corinthians 9:14: 'The Lord commanded that those who proclaim the gospel should get their living by the gospel.' This is the purpose of 6:6, extended from the preacher to the teacher: the pupil must share his goods with the teacher—i.e. must pay him for the work he has done.

This unexpected instruction, suddenly coming out of the blue, is then followed by an exhortation to honest thinking and generous doing. One of the ways in which we deceive ourselves is by thinking that God does not know everything and take everything into account. We think we can fool him. (The word means to turn up your nose at somebody.) This is not how it is with God, and we shall see that it is not when the last day comes and we stand before his judgment seat. On that day (the harvest, the end of the world) we shall 'reap' what we have sown. If, for example, we have spent an unnecessary amount of money on ourselves ('to your own flesh') we shall reap 'corruption' (i.e. God's condemnation); if we have been led by the Spirit into using money for the sake of other people (such as the teacher, mentioned in verse 6) God will reward us with 'eternal life' in the age to come.

This leads Paul to a general conclusion: he exhorts his Galatians to good works, for all and specially for those who belong to the church.

Written with his own hand

The major part of the letter, 1:1—6:10, has been dictated to a scribe; the rest of it, 6:11–18, Paul will write with his own hand. Notice that the last instruction that he gives them in the dictated part of the letter is to work: 'Let us work for the good of all.' Far too often, faith has been contrasted with works, as though the believer, the person of faith, was a 'non-doer'; and this way of thinking has been attributed to Paul. In fact, Paul exhorts his hearers to do things and he believes in a God who rewards works that have been performed in love.

Paul's contrast was between the works commanded by the Law (e.g. circumcision, dietary laws, the festivals and sabbaths) and works of love and faith. His final command is to work, while there is still time, and before the Lord comes and time is ended. There is nothing un-Pauline about activity; he was an example of what he taught.

PRAYER

Let us not deceive ourselves.
We cannot fool you.
Make us doers of the word.

NEW CREATION

Paul's handwriting, which began at this point in the original letter, is larger than that of his scribe. He takes over, to compose a summary of the whole argument and to authenticate the letter. (Compare the end of 2 Thessalonians (3:17): 'I, Paul, write this greeting with my own hand. This is the mark in every letter of mine; it is the way I write.' For the name of one of his scribes, see Romans 16:22.)

The motives of the troublemakers, he says, are purely selfish: they want the approval of others and they want to avoid persecution. Like Paul (5:11), they would be persecuted if they preached the cross of Christ, for such preaching implies the end of the Law and the unbelief of those who keep it.

Then he says that 'even the circumcised do not themselves obey the Law', possibly meaning that his opponents in Galatia are not themselves as perfect in their observances as they should be—or as he had been in the past, when he was 'far more zealous' than many of his contemporaries 'for the traditions of his ancestors' (1:14). He was an expert; they are mere amateurs. And their motivation is this: they can boast about the number of converts they have made, converts to a system that he denigrates as 'flesh'.

Shame becomes glory

Paul's life, as he showed us at the beginning of the letter, fell into two parts: before his conversion and after. The turning point was God's revelation of his Son; the one who had been crucified was the Lord. For Paul to change was like death and resurrection: the world was crucified to him, and he to the world (compare 2:19). All his ideas about God and how to live have been changed. He can no longer boast about converts and numbers as (he says) his opponents are doing. He can only boast about the cross. What before looked like shame is now seen to be God's glory. Weakness is strength, foolishness is wisdom. It is a 'new creation' that he is living in. He prays for peace and mercy upon those who see what he says and live by it: they are God's Israel, the true people of God. (This seems to be the meaning here, but it is much disputed; see REB footnote.)

Paul lived through a revolution and came out the other side a changed man. His priorities were altered and everything was turned upside-down. His letter to the Galatians is an attempt to share his understanding with others, and if he is at times very outspoken and extremely blunt, it's understandable.

To have read his letter is to have been invited to think his thoughts after him and to share his new insights. He has invited everyone who hears what he is saying to live the life of a new creation in what remains of the old.

PRAYER

'I have been crucified with Christ.'
May I never forget that!
Make me live to you.

The GUARANTEE of GENUINENESS

Paul's final sentences sum up much of the argument of the letter as a whole and leave the readers (or hearers) of it where he wants them to be—not where they were going before he began to write and they to hear what he had written.

There is no doubt that he has been troubled by the situation: it has aroused his anger and driven him to speak his mind. 'From now on' he hopes no one need raise these questions (of the observance of the Law by Gentile believers) again. He has given them the answer. But if they do still question him he has the final irrefutable reply for all to see, in the marks made in his flesh. He had been beaten with the thirty-nine lashes, five times; this was the punishment administered in synagogues. He had also been the victim of a stoning (2 Corinthians 11:24–25). You could see it, if you looked at him; and that was the proof that he no longer preached the Law. He was now the servant of Jesus—and he preached the cross, and was persecuted for it. His scars were his guarantee.

He will tell the Corinthians, later, about people who came to Corinth with letters of recommendation (2 Corinthians 3:1)—written evidence from someone else that they were genuine. He carries his recommendation on his back and in his skin: he has been punished in the synagogues. He has changed from Law-keeper to gospel-preacher and the evidence is his rejection by those who used to be his associates.

New creation

He had said that there was a new creation (6:15); in it, everything is upside-down. Rejection is acceptance, failure to persuade is proof of success; humiliation is honour.

This is how it had been with Jesus, and the slave of Jesus is marked with the same signs. Paul will develop this line of argument in a later letter to Corinth (2 Corinthians). Here, he leaves the whole matter like a time-bomb waiting to go off. Everyone reading 6:17 can work it out for themselves.

In conclusion he prays for them to live in 'the grace of our Lord Jesus Christ'—his favour, which is also God's favour. This is to fill their 'spirits'—and they need no longer worry about the flesh. They are his 'brothers and sisters', even though they have been foolish, bewitched, unsettled and on the edge of falling away from Christ. He is confident that his letter will keep them in God's love.

PRAYER

Thank you for Paul, his clarity and persuasiveness.
Thank you for Christ, his love and his grace.
Thank you for your knowledge of us.

PBC 1 AND 2 THESSALONIANS:
INTRODUCTION

Which is the earliest Christian writing? It is a question that interests us today. We want to know how things began, who was the first person to do something, which is the oldest example of something that eventually became common.

The only reference to Jesus writing is in a story that was eventually included in some manuscripts of John's Gospel (7:53—8:11). That was writing in the dust, however, and nothing else from his hand has survived, or even been attributed to him. He worked through people, not through books.

The books at the beginning of the New Testament, the four gospels, are generally thought to have been written between AD70 and AD100. But these are probably not the oldest books in the New Testament. The oldest books are almost certainly the letters of Paul.

We cannot be sure that we know the order in which they were written, but a good case can be made for thinking that the first letter to the Thessalonians is the earliest of Paul's letters that has survived. If so, it is the oldest example of Christian writing.

Even that statement needs to be qualified, because we do not have the actual handwritten letter that Paul, Silvanus and Timothy sent to Thessalonica. What we have is copies made from copies, all of them slightly different from each other; and we have to choose which version seems to be the oldest and most authentic. Fortunately, this problem does not arise very often in the case of 1 and 2 Thessalonians; most modern translations have notes to explain where there is an important variant reading (i.e. a place where the manuscripts disagree with one another), and there are very few in these letters. The Revised English Bible (1989) has none for 1 Thessalonians, and only one for 2 Thessalonians (2:13). The New Revised Standard Version has a total of nine for the two letters.

Not all Christian writings of the early years survived. We know, for example, that the Corinthians wrote to Paul, because he says so: 'Now concerning the matters about which you wrote...' (1 Corinthians 7:1). But their letter to him has not been kept, only his reply to it. It may be that the same thing happened in the case of 1 Thessalonians. Paul had sent Timothy to Thessalonica after he himself had left that city, to find out how the church was faring in difficult times; and it is possible that Timothy brought back to Paul not only an oral account of how they were but also a letter from the Thessalonians in which they asked Paul for teaching on some questions about which they were uncertain (see 1 Thessalonians 4:9—5:11). If that is what happened, then the lost letter from Thessalonica to Paul was earlier than Paul's first letter to the Thessalonians. We might say that it was almost the earliest Christian writing for which we have any kind of evidence—earlier still was the letter from the church in Jerusalem after the meeting described in Acts 15 (vv. 23–29).

Letters are substitutes for physical presence. Paul writes, like anyone else, because he is too far away from his audience for his voice to be heard. His letters were preserved at a time when other Christian writings were not preserved, because people regarded what Paul had written as important, too important to be thrown away. Even his opponents (and, as we shall see, he had many who disagreed with him) said as much: 'His letters ... are weighty and powerful.'

However, they went on to say, 'But when he is present he is unimpressive, and as a speaker he is beneath contempt' (2 Corinthians 10:10, REB). Paul denied this charge. It cannot have been true. We know from his letter to the Galatians that the reason he stayed there on his first visit, and preached the gospel to them, was that he was ill. But even so, the Galatians had welcomed him as if he were an angel of God, or Christ Jesus himself (Galatians 4:12–14). His critics were right, however, about the letters: they are weighty and powerful. They were the earliest writings that the churches collected, and they have continued to be used in churches ever since.

The actual date of writing 1 Thessalonians is usually reckoned to be about AD50, and 2 Thessalonians soon after, though more needs to be said about this second letter. The place where Paul was when he wrote these letters was either Athens (see 1 Thessalonians 3) or Corinth, the city to which he went after Athens. For this period of Paul's life, see also the accounts in Acts 17 and 18.

Most of Paul's letters were written because of confusion and conflict in the church that he was addressing in the letter: Paul had heard about the problem, and was unable to travel to the place concerned, so he wrote instead. As he founded more and more groups of believers, in what is now Turkey and Greece, it must have become an ever-increasing burden. He refers to it when he lists the troubles that are wearing him out: 'Apart from these external things [i.e. accidents that have happened to him—he seems to have been accident-prone] there is the responsibility that weighs on me every day, my anxious concern for all the churches. Is anyone weak? I share his weakness. If anyone brings about the downfall of another does my heart not burn with anger?' (2 Corinthians 11:28, 29, REB)

In the case of 1 Thessalonians, the situation seems to have been slightly different from what came to be the pattern elsewhere in the later letters. Paul does not rebuke troublemakers, as he does in Galatians, Corinthians, Philippians, Colossians and Romans. There is a hint, towards the end of the letter, that there are people who must be admonished; he refers to them as the idlers (1 Thessalonians 5:14), and there will be further references to them in the second letter (2 Thessalonians 3:6–12).

Why, then, did Paul write the first letter? He had gone to Thessalonica from Philippi, where he had suffered and been outrageously treated (1 Thessalonians 2:2); but he had preached the gospel in Thessalonica in face of great opposition, and had then departed, suddenly (by night, according to the account in Acts 17:1–10). He had wanted to return to Thessalonica, but had been prevented (1 Thessalonians 2:17–20); so eventually he had sent Timothy to find out how they were and to encourage them (1 Thessalonians 3:1–5). Timothy returned with a good report (and perhaps a letter from the Thessalonians to Paul) and Paul writes 1 Thessalonians in much joy and with many references to thanksgiving (1 Thessalonians 3:6–13). Thus he says, 'We always thank God for you all' (1:2); 'We have reason to thank God continually' (2:13); 'What thanks can we give to God in return for you? What thanks for all the joy you have brought us, making us rejoice before our God?' (3:9, REB).

Thus the earliest surviving example of Christian literature was motivated by joy; and the joy that motivated Paul was the result, he believed, of what God had done and was continuing to do in Thessalonica. God had given the Thessalonians the gifts of faith and love and hope; and he had sustained them in the maintenance of this life, in spite of the troubles that had come upon them. Later, when Paul wrote to the Galatians, he gave them a list of the fruit of the Spirit, and he put joy near the top of it, second only to love.

What was the cause of the trouble in Thessalonica? The author of the Acts of the Apostles says that it was brought on by the members of the Jewish synagogue (Acts 17:5–8), and this may be borne out by a passage in 1 Thessalonians (2:14–16) in which Paul describes the trouble that 'the Jews' have caused to the churches in Judea, and draws a parallel with what is happening in Thessalonica. This is the usual view of the origins of the trouble in Thessalonica.

It is possible, however, that Acts is slightly misleading at this point. The author of Acts seems to gloss over the differences between Paul and the church in Jerusalem, making it look as though everything was settled at the meeting there, described in Acts 15. We know from Paul's letters that conflict continued—in Galatia, Corinth, Rome and Philippi. It may be that 'the Jews' who caused trouble in Thessalonica were Jewish Christians, who had come from Jerusalem to Thessalonica to preach a different gospel from that which Paul preached. Compare what Paul says about his opponents in Corinth: 'Are they Hebrews? So am I. Israelites? So am I. Abraham's descendants? So am I. Are they servants of Christ? I am mad to speak like this, but I can outdo them...' (2 Corinthians 11:22–27, REB).

It is regrettable that the word 'panacea' is generally used in a derogatory sense, as if there were no such thing as a cure for all ills, as if all panaceas were delusions. Paul would not have agreed with that. He tells the Thessalonians to rejoice always, and to give thanks in all circumstances (1 Thessalonians 5:16, 18). He believed that the gospel that he had preached and that they had received was the cure for all ills, making it possible to rejoice and give thanks, whatever the situation you found yourself in. The oldest surviving Christian document is an assurance of the complete and universal effectiveness of Christian faith.

The second letter to the Thessalonians raises more problems than the first. The chief of these is: did Paul write it? That may seem an odd question to ask when there is so much in 2 Thessalonians that says it is by Paul and his two companions, Silvanus and Timothy—for example, the first words at the beginning of the letter, and the final two verses in Paul's handwriting: 'I, Paul, write this greeting with my own hand. This is the mark in every letter of mine; it is the way I write. The grace of our Lord Jesus Christ be with all of you' (2 Thessalonians 3:17, 18; compare Galatians 6:11–18, also written in his own hand). There is also the reminder of Paul's example of not accepting expenses or free accommodation (2 Thessalonians 3:6–15), and the remarkable closeness of structure and wording between the two letters, which assumes that they were written within a short period of time, when Paul, Silvanus and Timothy were all three together in one place.

Nevertheless, the Pauline authorship of 2 Thessalonians has often been doubted. It does seem to be the case that letters were written as if by Paul on matters to do with church discipline and Christian faith; the two letters to Timothy and the letter to Titus are often thought to be by a later writer. There is a letter attributed to Barnabas which is included in a mid-fourth-century manuscript of the New Testament, *Codex Sinaiticus*, and it is usually regarded as a second-century writing, not by the apostle Barnabas. Attitudes to authorship were different in the ancient world (and in the early church) from what they are today.

The content of 2 Thessalonians, with its detailed predictions concerning the return of Christ, is not quite like anything Paul says elsewhere in his surviving letters. So the suggestion has been made that a later writer used 1 Thessalonians as an outline, adapting the structure and wording of that letter, to compose a second letter that would deal with a new situation. This later writer would have believed that he was adapting the insights and methods of Paul to the problem of his own day, when people were claiming that the day of the Lord was already present, and were saying that Paul himself had said so. (A similar explanation is sometimes given to account for the relationship between Colossians and Ephesians.)

Whether we take the view that Paul wrote 2 Thessalonians, or whether we think it was written by an adapter (the present writer is slightly inclined to the former view), the existence of the second letter to the Thessalonians is evidence of some of the problems that existed in the early church. What are we to think about the second coming? What did Paul really mean? Which letters did he write? All of these were questions that arose, whichever view we take of the authorship of 2 Thessalonians.

If 'joy in all circumstances' is the theme of 1 Thessalonians, 'the hope of glory' is the theme of 2 Thessalonians. The mistake that has been made by some members of the congregation in Thessalonica is to think that God has nothing further in store for his creatures. He has infinitely more: he will give them the glory of our Lord Jesus Christ (2 Thessalonians 2:14). What is still waiting to be revealed to us and obtained by us is the splendour that has already been given to Jesus; he now shares the status of God. The Father and the Son are spoken of in the same breath (2 Thessalonians 1:1; 2:16). The future will be unimaginably wonderful, far surpassing even the joy that is ours in the present.

Quotations are taken from the New Revised Standard Version (Anglicized Edition) (NRSV), 1989, unless otherwise indicated. The other translation that has been most frequently used is the Revised English Bible (REB), 1989.

Suggestions for further reading

There are two fairly recent commentaries on the Thessalonian letters:

F.F. Bruce, *1 & 2 Thessalonians*, Word Biblical Commentary, Volume 45 (Word Books, 1982)

I. Howard Marshall, *1 & 2 Thessalonians*, The New Century Bible Commentary (Wm. B. Eerdmans and Marshall Morgan and Scott Publishers Ltd, 1983)

Two other books may also be mentioned here:

Maarten J.J. Menken, *2 Thessalonians* (Routledge, 1994)

Michael Goulder, *A Tale of Two Missions* (SCM Press, 1994)

In GOD

The letter opens in the usual way, with the names of the three who are sending it (Paul, Silvanus and Timothy) first, and then those to whom it is addressed: the church of the Thessalonians. This was the normal form for letters at that time, both public letters and private, both secular and religious. What is remarkable, however, is what is said next—that the church of the Thessalonians is in God the Father and the Lord Jesus Christ.

The opening of 2 Thessalonians is almost exactly the same as this, but in no other letter of Paul, nor in any other letter in the New Testament, is it said at the beginning that the church is 'in God'. Paul frequently uses the expression 'in Christ', but seldom 'in God'. Here and in 2 Thessalonians the two expressions are combined: the church is both in God and in Christ. The 'place' where the church exists is where God the Father and Jesus both are.

Just as birds exist in the air, fish in the sea, worms in the earth and coals in the fire, so also the element in which the church lives is God. Apart from God, the church would be inexplicable; it would consist entirely of deluded people, sadly misled by events and waiting expectantly for hopes that would never be fulfilled. The church makes no sense at all, if there is no God.

Believing in the church

We say in the creed that we believe in the church; it comes towards the end of the creed, after we have said that we believe in God the Father, the Son and the Holy Spirit. Just as they are known by faith, and not by sight, so too the church is an object of faith. Can we really say that this group of people, meeting in this building at some time each week, is 'in God', and that he is the element essential for their existence? Without him they would be like birds that could not fly, fish out of water, worms without soil, or coals that had burnt out. Can we believe that God is the cause of their meeting, the power that sustains and preserves them and makes them unlike any other meeting, because they are 'in God' in a way that none other is? What sort of evidence is there for this?

It would be a simple matter to list all the characteristics of a group of Christian believers that suggest they have no connection with God whatsoever: quarrelling, self-importance, distrust, fear, habit, nostalgia, antiquarianism and so on. None of these would move us to say, 'These people are in God.'

To say that, we should have to know them better. Then we would find extraordinary faith that kept them going, love for other people that led them to do unexpected acts of kindness, and confidence that life had a good purpose, no matter what happened to them. Even the bare fact that they continued to meet could be explained in more than one way; if it were a mistake, it was a mistake that lasted for a long time.

As we read these letters to the Thessalonians, we shall see further what it means to be 'in God'. We shall understand more clearly what to look for in the church—what has started it; what is its element and its essential life; what it means to be a member of it.

PRAYER

Thank you for Paul and his companions.
Thank you for the church of the Thessalonians.
Thank you that the church exists in you.

FAITH, LOVE & HOPE

What Paul has already said, in the opening words of his letter, reminds his readers that the church not only belongs to God, but also exists in him: it is in God the Father and the Lord Jesus Christ. What Paul says next draws out some of the consequences of this.

The first of these is that Paul thanks God for the Thessalonian congregation, realizing that they are the work of God, for which God is responsible. The church exists entirely because of God. Nothing could be in him, without his willing it to be there. God had decided that there should be a church of Thessalonians; and because God came first in Thessalonica, thanksgiving must come first in Paul's letter, as also in his life. Hence he says, 'We always give thanks to God for all of you.' It was a happy accident that the normal pattern of a letter, in the first century AD, went from address to thanksgiving, and Paul follows this custom in every letter of his that has survived, except the one he wrote to the Galatians, where the situation was such that instead of 'I thank God', he says, 'I am astonished' (Galatians 1:6).

Praying for the church

The second consequence of Paul's insight that the church exists in God is that he prays for it: 'We ... mention you in our prayers.' It would be foolish to think that if the church is in God, we do not need to pray for it. We are to pray for God's will to be done; the fact that something is God's will does not exclude us from praying first. Just the opposite: we pray *because* it is his will. The reason why this is so is that God is love, and love insists on sharing everything; prayer is one of the ways in which we co-operate with God in getting his will done.

Paul then tells the Thessalonians what it is that he mentioned in his prayers for them. To do this, he makes use of a formula that sums up all the various aspects of what it is to be a member of the church; it can all be expressed under three headings: faith, love and hope. He will use the formula again later in this letter (5:8) and, with a minor variation, in the second letter (faith, love and steadfastness—2 Thessalonians 1:3, 4; see also 1 Corinthians 13:13; Galatians 5:5, 6; Colossians 1:4, 5). The usual order is first faith, which refers to God's actions in the past, above all in raising Jesus from the dead; second love, which relates to those who are with us in the present; third hope, which looks forward to the future. It is only in 1 Corinthians 13:13 that Paul varies the order in order to place love at the climax of the series.

God has given the Thessalonians the grace to have faith, to love and to hope. It is by these three activities that they stand with Paul before our God and Father.

To each of these three activities Paul attaches a word to describe what it is that is characteristic of the action: faith enables them to work, love to labour, and hope to be steadfast, to endure. There is no suggestion here or elsewhere in Paul that being believers means we no longer do things. The frequent and popular contrast between faith and works is misleading and bears no relation to Paul's teaching. Faith, if it is genuine, expresses itself in the performance of works that are inevitable and appropriate; believers are recognizable by what they do. Similarly with love: you cannot love without being involved in the labours of love. Hope, too, expresses itself in endurance: it is living out of the future—the time when Christ will return to judge the living and the dead and to initiate the new age on the earth. This manifests itself in confidence about the future and in willingness to wait and to put up with trials and tribulations in the meantime.

All Christian living is comprehended in three words: faith, love and hope.

PRAYER

Thank you for the gift of faith, by which we work.
Thank you for the gift of love, by which we labour.
Thank you for the gift of hope, by which we endure.

I CHOSE YOU

One of the characteristics of Paul's writing that makes him so accessible to readers today is that he bases what he says on facts that can be established without any doubt. He is certainly not afraid to make great claims (both for his readers and for himself), but he knows what reasons he has for saying these things, and he does not fail to mention them. His theology is rooted in events—events that have taken place in his own experience and in the experience of those to whom he is writing. See, for example, a passage in the letter to the Galatians (3:2), where he says that there is one argument that will settle the whole issue: what were you doing when you received the Spirit?

Paul has already made the astonishing claim that the meeting of the Thessalonians to which he is writing is 'in God': they have faith and love and hope; they are unlike any other association of people in the city of Thessalonica, in that they believe in God as the Father of Jesus Christ; they are committed to one another in love; and they are waiting for the coming of Jesus Christ, the resurrection of the dead, the judgment, and the life of the age to come. These are facts that anyone can observe; Paul believes that they point to what God thinks about them, and what God has done for them.

Chosen by God

He goes back to the beginning, as he will later on, when he is writing to the Galatians. The Thessalonians are loved by God; God has chosen them. As in the Gospel of John, the truth of the matter is not that believers have chosen God, but that God has chosen them (John 15:16). This is what any believer is driven to say. It would be totally wrong to say, 'I chose to believe', because that is not how it is; faith is experienced as a gift that has been received, a present that has been thrust upon you, something that happened to you rather than something you sought or chose. To say, 'I chose to believe', and leave it at that, might imply that you were in some way superior to others who had not made the same choice—more clear-sighted, more honest and intelligent, a better person. This is the last thing any believer wants to claim.

The language of choice, election, predestination and so on has to be used with caution. Properly understood, it has only one meaning: it refers to how those who believe understand themselves. The most characteristic Christian verbs are used in the passive: for example (as the hymn by H.F. Lyte puts it), 'ransomed, healed, restored, forgiven'. The mistake is to turn these words round in order to say things about other people—that they are *not* chosen, *not* forgiven, but predestined to damnation. The words are valid in the positive, but not in the negative. We know about belief, not about unbelief.

In spite of the difficulties and misunderstandings, both Jews and Christians have found themselves forced into the use of the vocabulary of election and predestination, in order to express the sense of sheer grace, unworthiness, gratitude and thanks for what has happened.

But Paul will not leave the matter of God's prevenient love and choice, without reminding his readers of the evidence on which what he has said is based. 'Our message of the gospel', that is, what happened when he and Silvanus and Timothy preached in Thessalonica, was not just a matter of words spoken into the air. The preaching was effective, and had a powerful influence on the Thessalonians: they received the Spirit, they were fully convinced that what they heard was true. Paul did not need to list the events that followed; his readers knew them perfectly well—miracles, speaking with tongues, lives changed, and so on.

The Thessalonians came to the same conclusion as the Galatians had done already: the Galatians had welcomed Paul as an angel of God, as Jesus Christ (Galatians 4:14). In Thessalonica, too, Paul and his companions were recognized as people who were the servants of those to whom they preached; they accepted no expenses, but worked to earn money in order not to be a burden to the new church (see 2 Thessalonians 3:6–12).

PRAYER

Thank you for those who brought the gospel to us.
Thank you for the conviction you gave us that it was true.
Thank you for your love for us, and your choice of us.

The GOSPEL

Six times in this letter, Paul refers to 'the gospel' (1:5; 2:2, 4, 8, 9; 3:2). When he uses the word, he does not mean a book; he is not referring to one of the four Gospels in the New Testament, or to any other written source. The literal meaning of the Greek word is 'good news', and that is the sense in which Paul uses it. Notice how he uses the verb 'to bring good news' in this way: 'Timothy has just now come to us from you, and has brought us the good news of your faith and love' (3:6).

Because the Greek word could refer to any good news, Paul sometimes adds 'of God' or 'of Christ': it is the good news that Christ died for us, and that God raised him from the dead (1 Corinthians 15:3, 4). This is the centre of all that Paul says in his letters; it is the authority to which he appeals. All that he knows about God, Christ, the Spirit and the church is derived from the gospel. Paul had received it and he handed it on, through preaching and teaching, and in his letters also. The Greek word is *evangelion*, and it is the origin of our words 'evangelist' and 'evangelical'.

Jesus died and lives

The central reference point for many later Christian writers has been the life and teaching of Jesus—what he said and did before he was put to death in Jerusalem. This was not how Paul wrote in his letters. In them, he never refers to the healing miracles, the parables of Jesus, the events at the time of his birth, the transfiguration, and so on. On a very few occasions, in his surviving letters, he quotes and refers to the sayings of Jesus. (See, for example, 4:15 below for one possible instance of this.) When Paul uses the expression 'the life of Jesus' (2 Corinthians 4:10, 11), he means the life that began at the resurrection, not the life that ended at the crucifixion. Whereas we might say of someone, 'He lived and died', Paul puts it the other way round: 'Jesus died and lives.'

Thus the gospel of God (or of Christ) is to do with the Lord who gave himself up to death for others, and is now alive for ever through God's power. Faith in this makes discipleship possible, and love for other Christian brothers and sisters, and hope, which is waiting for Christ's return and for God's unending rule, his kingdom.

Each of the four books we call 'Gospels' may have had, as its heading, 'The Gospel according to Mark', or 'Matthew', or 'Luke', or 'John'. There was one gospel, one good news, now contained in four different books. Gradually, however, the word 'gospel' came to mean the book itself, rather than the message that the book contained; so people began to speak of 'four Gospels'. But this was many years after the death of Paul, so with him, 'gospel' never means a book—they were almost certainly not written in his lifetime—but always the message, the good news, of the death and resurrection of Jesus.

PRAYER

We believe in the resurrection of the dead.
Thank you for the gift of eternal life.
Thank you for what Christ has done,
and what you have done through him.
Gospel means Good News.
Whatever we are feeling, that is still true.
Thank you for that.

The REVOLUTION *of* FAITH

Paul continues to remind his readers in Thessalonica of what happened when he and his two companions preached the gospel there. The result of the preaching was evidence of God's approval of the believers; God had worked a miracle in the lives of the Thessalonians by changing their minds and this had become known to others in that part of the world.

Paul's argument is still that faith is strengthened by reflecting on experience; what happened to us is best explained as the action of God.

The particular point made here is that though the believers become the object of other people's hatred, though they were persecuted, they were nevertheless filled with joy. Suffering co-existed with joy. In most circumstances we would expect ill-treatment to produce sadness and misery; the normal person wants to be popular, and resents and avoids scorn. But it was not so when the gospel was preached in Thessalonica; the Holy Spirit imparted joy to those who believed the good news, even when they were being ill-used by others.

Paul and his companions had been maltreated in Philippi, when they were on the way to Thessalonica (see 1 Thessalonians 2:1, 2), so the Thessalonians knew what to expect. Then they found themselves in the same situation. Both they and those who preached to them were following the pattern of the Lord himself. The preaching concerned Christ crucified, and it was the opposite of everyday wisdom which said that in order to be joyful you must be comfortable and successful. Paul will say later that the gospel is the word of God, not a human word (1 Thessalonians 2:13): it tells us things that we would not otherwise know. One of these things is that it is possible (necessary, in fact) to be joyful on all occasions and in all circumstances. Paul will say so, explicitly, at the end of this letter: 'Rejoice always' (1 Thessalonians 5:16).

Finding joy

The gospel contradicts worldly wisdom. It involves the story of someone who failed to persuade others to follow him, was isolated from his friends, died in darkness and disgrace, mocked to death by the authorities, and who thought himself abandoned by God who had turned his face against him (see Mark 15). This is the saving event, the way in which God acts in the world. It teaches us to disconnect the search for joy from what we imagine to be self-fulfilment, but to find it instead in what destroys our plans and frustrates our hopes and expectations. What we thought impossible—joy, and the annihilation of self-will—turns out not to be so; blessedness is to be found in having nothing.

The faith that can accept this stands out in an otherwise drab and worldly world of pleasure-seeking and competitiveness. It is so unusual that it cannot go unnoticed. All over Macedonia and Achaia, other believers have heard about the joy of the persecuted Thessalonians, and been encouraged by it. The faith of one church is strengthened by hearing about the faith of another. Faith feeds on faith and is nourished by it.

Paul had used the expression earlier, '...your work of faith' (1:3), and this may be an example of what faith does. It works by turning things into their opposites. (Paul will give a list of them in 2 Corinthians 6:8–10.) What we had most feared, and thus tried to avoid, becomes what we prize most highly; what we had dreaded is welcomed; what we hoped to escape is accepted. Faith turns minuses into pluses, and pluses into minuses. The first are last, and the last first.

PRAYER

Give me faith to see everything in reverse:
to accept what I now resist;
to want to be nothing myself, but you to be everything.

From IDOLS to GOD

What happened in Thessalonica when the gospel was preached there has become the talk not only of people in Macedonia (e.g. Philippi) and Achaia (e.g. Athens and Corinth), but of everyone who has heard about it. Paul describes what has been reported as 'the word of the Lord', and he says that what is happening has relieved him and his companions of any need to speak about it themselves. The account of how people believed the gospel is itself a presentation of the gospel. Faith lived is a proclamation of faith.

This may explain a remarkable fact about the New Testament. In all the exhortations in the various letters that it contains, there is hardly any instruction to a congregation to preach, or spread the gospel, or make converts in the place where they live. Paul accuses the Corinthians of most sins, but never of failing in the missionary strategy and evangelistic outreach. Perhaps it was recognized that living by faith was infectious; the good news could be caught as well as taught.

Of course there was still need for words; the Thessalonians would never have believed had not Paul and Silvanus and Timothy spoken. But speech is not the only means of evangelization: the lives of the believers and the existence of the congregation to which they belong are visible evidence of the power of God.

Listen to the evidence

As so often in his letters, having made a claim Paul immediately explains what has happened; the evidence that supports the claim is supplied. Apparently the majority of believers in Thessalonica had been Gentiles before they became Christians—Gentiles and not Jews. They had been accustomed to worshipping their gods, using idols— statues that represented the deity in which they believed. In the ancient world, Jews alone had no such aids to worship. One of the Ten Commandments had forbidden it: 'You shall not make for yourself an idol... You shall not bow down to them or worship them' (Exodus 20:4, 5).

Christianity, which began in an entirely Jewish setting, carried on the tradition of not having three-dimensional images of God, or of

Christ, for many centuries, and in the Eastern churches this is still the case—all icons are 'flat'.

There is much to be said for not representing God by any visible form, flat or carved. The prohibition of idols of any kind corresponds with the belief that God is unlike everything else; he is the creator of everything, therefore no creature can adequately, or even inadequately, represent him. The absence of a statue of God in the temple at Jerusalem, which surprised those who were not Jews and expected him to be represented by an image, tells us something about Jewish (and Christian) belief in God. The God of Israel is, it is believed, the living and true God, and is more different from everything imaginable than all imaginable things are from one another. No object, with length, breadth, height, mass and location, can signify him, precisely because it is an object and invites us to see it in the round and visit it in its place.

The Thessalonian converts were reported as having turned away from idols of God, to serve him—the God who lives (unlike an idol) and is the only God that there is. An idol would be a representation of something we could use; God is known as the one to whom everyone is a servant; he is never an object, but always the subject.

PRAYER

Turn me from idols.
Turn me from self-serving.
Turn me to serve you.

The HOPE *of* SALVATION

The section of the letter that began in verse 2 referred to the faith, love and hope of the Thessalonians. It then went on to describe their faith—how God had given them the ability to believe in the gospel that Paul and his companions had preached. Now, as we come to the end of this section, it is rounded off with a further statement about their hope: they began to wait for God's Son to come from heaven. Hope is living out of the future, confident about what will happen. Jesus, they believed, would return in glory; and the last judgment would follow, and the life of the age to come.

The earliest disciples believed themselves to be living on the edge of the new age. The resurrection of Jesus was the beginning of what was to happen universally: it had been predicted in the book of Daniel that, after the time of anguish, many of those who slept in the dust of the earth would awake, some to everlasting life, and some to shame and everlasting contempt (Daniel 12:1, 2). The resurrection of Jesus, they believed, must be the beginning of the general resurrection; he was the first fruits of those who had died (1 Corinthians 15:20). God would then rule on the earth in a way that he had not done since the disobedience of Adam and Eve in the garden (Genesis 3). Creation would be set free from its bondage to decay, and would obtain the freedom of the glory of the children of God (Romans 8:21). Death, the last enemy, would be destroyed (1 Corinthians 15:26).

The angel had told Daniel that some would enter everlasting life, and others would rise to shame and everlasting contempt. The division would take place at the last judgment, and Jesus, so the Christians believed, would be God's agent who would sit on the judgment seat (2 Corinthians 5:10).

The first Christians not only believed that this would happen soon, they also longed for it to happen, and prayed that it would. Perhaps the oldest Christian prayer that we know is *Marana tha*, 'Our Lord, come!' (1 Corinthians 16:22) This must strike us as strange; we should be more likely to ask God to give us time to repent and adjust our lives so as to be more prepared for judgment and the new world. But that was not how they thought—neither the first Christians in the earliest days of the church, nor some, at least, later in the first century, who were still praying, 'Come, Lord Jesus!' (Revelation 22:20)

Living without fear

An essential component of Christian faith was that God had given the believers advance information that they would be acquitted at the judgment. This was what was meant when it was said that Christ was raised for our justification (Romans 4:25). They could, therefore, live without fear; the future contained nothing that made them anxious. They believed themselves to be those who were destined for eternal life.

The Son for whom they waited would be not only the judge but also the one who rescued them from the wrath that was coming— that is, from the condemnation of God at the judgment. He had associated people with himself, during the time before his death in Jerusalem. When anyone asked, 'What must I do to inherit eternal life?' the answer had been, 'Follow me' (Mark 10:17–22). It was exactly the same now. If the question were asked in the form, 'What must I do to be saved?' the answer was 'Believe on the Lord Jesus, and you will be saved, you and your household' (Acts 16:30, 31).

In Paul's letters, the words 'save' and 'salvation' were nearly always used of this future for which the Christians were waiting. It was thought of not primarily as the experience of individuals, but as the renewal of all things, through the lifting of the curse imposed in Eden. Salvation is nearer to us now than when we became believers (Romans 13:11). It was the time to be prayed for and longed for, because God would be everything to everybody (1 Corinthians 15:28).

PRAYER

Finish your new creation.
Let us see your great salvation.
Be everything to everyone.

WAITING *for* HIS SON

The first Christians about whom we have any evidence believed that they were living between two critical moments in the history of the world: the first was the death and resurrection of Jesus, which for them was in the recent past; the second was the return of Jesus from heaven, to judge the world, and they expected this to happen in the immediate future.

They used both of these moments as ways of describing themselves. Paul, for example, refers to a fellow Christian as 'one for whom Christ died' (Romans 14:15); and here in 1 Thessalonians he describes them as waiting for God's Son to come from heaven. Further on in this letter he will distinguish between those who will have died before the return of Jesus, and others whom he describes as 'we who are alive, who are left until the coming of the Lord' (4:15).

Temporary world

The coming of Jesus from heaven did not happen in their lifetime, as they had expected it to. Nevertheless, waiting for something is still an aspect of the Christian life that we cannot give up. To think of anything in the present world as if it were permanent, eternal, would be to make an idol of it. Everything that we have is temporary and provisional, and must be treated as such.

The temptation to idolize people and things is with us all the time, but especially in a period when there are rapid changes in the way we live. In reaction against these changes we are tempted to cling to the past and retain something from it in preference to anything new—because the old is better, for no other reason than that it is old.

The appropriate stance for the Christian believer is forward-looking, expectant, regarding the past and the present as time to be endured, and longing for God's promises to be fulfilled in the future. 'Salvation is nearer to us now than when we became believers' (Romans 13:11). There is not much room for faith or hope in nostalgia.

The first and second letters to the Thessalonians have more to say about what is still to happen, and are less concerned about the past. They remind us that we are travellers, pilgrims, passing through, on the way to a better country. We ignore this element in the New

Testment at our peril. Faith has to say, 'Christ will come again. God will make all things new. He will succeed. He will hallow his name by making everything come right.'

PRAYER

Give us hope.

'For all that has been—thanks!
For all that shall be—Yes!'

Dag Hammarskjöld (*Markings*)

The WRATH *that is* COMING

Three times in this letter Paul refers to God's wrath (1:10; 2:16; 5:9). What he means by the expression is the opposite of salvation. These are the two sentences that will be passed at the last judgment: to those on God's right, salvation; to those on his left, condemnation. The picture was part of Paul's Jewish inheritance; the clearest statement of it in the New Testament is the parable of the sheep and the goats in Matthew 25:31–46.

A wise man had said, 'All things come in pairs, one opposite the other' (Ecclesiasticus 42:24). Salvation meant entry into the new age; its opposite, wrath, meant exclusion from it—*Gehenna* (literally, the name of a place near Jerusalem where rubbish was burnt). Our minds are such that it is almost impossible to think one without also thinking the other—as with so many other pairs: pass or fail, innocent or guilty, yes or no.

We are touching on a subject that has caused immense anxiety to some people—to those, that is, who have believed that they are bound to be the object of God's wrath at the last judgment. What can be said about it?

First, as someone pointed out, that it is proper, right and inevitable to think that if anyone is to be damned, it is only me. I can think of excellent excuses for everybody else, but not for me. Failures, omissions, cruelties, hatreds and so on; lack of kindness, generosity, gratitude, leave us in despair from time to time. It would be abnormal (or at any rate, arrogant) never to fear our own damnation.

Salvation, not damnation

Second, it is very noticeable how infrequently the subject comes up in the New Testament, or how even then it is mainly confined to a few books, such as Matthew's Gospel, Revelation, and some passages in Paul's letters. The reason for this comparative absence is that the first Christians were far more interested in salvation than in damnation. The gospel was all about being saved from the wrath of God. The subject came up in a negative way: we have been rescued from our condemnation; we have been justified, reconciled; we are at peace with God.

Third, faith has to fight, and to hold on to the good news; and to do this, it has to recognize that there could be bad news, which must be rejected. Faith is a choice: shall I see myself as a total disaster, or shall I dare to believe that I am redeemable? To choose the latter requires constant help, the grace to believe that there is mercy, and that justice is not the only way that God deals with us. Paul's reference to God's rescue of us from wrath is the good news we certainly need.

PRAYER

Thank you for Paul's faith in our salvation.
Thank you for the forgiveness of our sins.
Help us to forgive.

APPROVED *by* GOD

It seems from this passage that there were people in Thessalonica who were criticizing Paul and his companions, and that this is a reply to such criticism.

Paul reminds his readers in Thessalonica of what they know already about him and Silvanus and Timothy, and about the work that they had done in Thessalonica when they preached there. Their visit had borne fruit: the result of their preaching was the founding of the church, and that meant the existence of a group of people all of whom had gifts of the Spirit.

This followed on from a bad time for Paul and the others in Philippi, but that had not deterred them from preaching the same gospel again in Thessalonica, where there was also opposition to it. How was it that the missionaries continued to proclaim the good news, when it produced such violent reactions? Their encouragement came from God.

People are saying that the visitors are deceivers, deluded, interested only in themselves. But this is not so; they have God's approval, and they work in obedience to him. He is no easy-going lord and master—he knows our thoughts and keeps them under constant examination.

Notice how many references to God there are in these four verses: God gives courage; what is preached is the gospel of God; those who preach it have God's approval; they are always working under God's critical examination of them.

Who were the people who were criticizing Paul's mission in Thessalonica? We cannot be sure; Paul did not need to explain in his letter to the Thessalonians, because they already knew. Paul was writing for them, not for us.

It may have been people in Thessalonica who disliked the new movement that had so recently sprung up there. It may have been members of the Jewish synagogue who regarded the church as their rival. Or it may possibly have been people arriving in Thessalonica and claiming to have authority from James in Jerusalem, preaching a different gospel that involved keeping the whole of the Old Testament Law—the same group that seemed to have caused trouble in Galatia (e.g. 3:1; 5:7), Corinth (e.g. 2 Corinthians 11:22ff.), Rome (e.g. chs. 14 and 15) and elsewhere (e.g. Philippians 3:1–19).

God's agents

We cannot tell, but what we can see is that Paul's first reaction to these opponents is to refer to his (and his companions') relationship with God. God caused the mission to be fruitful; God saw to it that the opposition did not deter either the missionaries or the converts; God showed his approval of them in the fact of the church's existence; and God kept them under constant review.

This was no knock-down argument. The opponents could say that the preachers and their converts were simply deluded. How, otherwise, would you explain the indisputable fact of strange religions and misguided beliefs? Anyone could claim to have God's approval; nobody, and nothing, could prove that you had it.

This is certainly true. But what matters is something slightly different. What matters is that those who claim to be God's agents should continually test themselves by asking themselves this question: who am I trying to please—God, or those to whom I preach, or myself? We cannot know our motives completely or be sure why we do what we do. But at least we must see that what is important—the *only* thing that is important—is God's approval of us. This is the essential question, and we must continue to ask it, always hoping to find some sort of answer.

PRAYER

Keep me critical of myself.
Make me listen to the criticisms that people make of me.
Because all hearts are open to you, and all desires known.

GOD *who* TESTS OUR HEARTS

The heart meant something different to the people of the ancient world from what it means to us. And not only to the people of the ancient world; even until the seventeenth century no one knew that the main function of the heart was to distribute blood around the body by pumping it through the veins and arteries.

The heart was thought to be the part of the body where the mind functioned. People did not know that the brain was the seat of thought, but they supposed that they thought with their heart. This was why the hearts of kings and of other notable people were sometimes preserved in a separate place from the rest of their corpses. The heart was special: it was the real you.

In the Collect for Purity at the beginning of the Holy Communion service in the Book of Common Prayer, we ask that God, to whom all hearts are open, will cleanse the thoughts of our hearts; we mean that he knows what we think, and that we want him to change our minds from having evil thoughts to having good ones.

The emotions, it was held, had their location further down in the body, in the kidneys—the 'reins' as they are called in the old translations of the Psalms.

It might, therefore, be better to translate the Greek word *kardia* (i.e. heart) as 'mind' when, as here, Paul speaks of God who tests our hearts; he means that God knows our plans and intentions, what we really want, and he assesses them, weighs them up. He knows us inside out.

Strengthened in holiness

Later in this letter Paul contrasts physical absence from Thessalonica with abandonment of them: '...separated from you—in person, not in heart' (2:17). He had had to move on to another place in order to preach the gospel there, but he carried them with him in his thoughts. He prays that God will strengthen their hearts in holiness (3:13): that is, that they will want what God wants for them and do his will.

The importance of the heart or mind comes in the gospels. Mark records Jesus as saying that what defiles us and makes us unclean is not what we eat, but what comes from the heart: our thoughts and plans; the things we decide to do (7:21–23).

We cannot over-estimate the importance of thinking. It really matters what we think. Having bad thoughts and negative attitudes leads to all kinds of disruptive and destructive actions. The point where we need help is at the *source* of what we do—where we entertain evil thoughts. This is why we ask God to adjust our thinking, to turn our minds from anger, jealousy, envy and all the rest, to the good thoughts of what he wants from us.

PRAYER

Cleanse the thoughts of our hearts.
Cast out the evil from our minds.
Fill us with love, joy and peace.

On BEING LOVED

The point is still being made that the readers of the letter have the facts, if only they will reflect on them. Because the preachers (i.e. Paul, Silvanus and Timothy) are sure of what happened in Thessalonica, they can call on God to bear witness: they are not afraid of the facts and so can speak on oath.

We are overhearing people who are involved in a row. Some are saying that the missionaries are deceivers, in it for what they can get out of it, and it seems as though there are enough people in Thessalonica who will believe this charge, to make it necessary for the letter to rebut it.

Can they not distinguish between self-seeking and genuine affection? That is the issue. Paul and his companions are horrified that the Thessalonians are willing to allow people to say that he and his friends are cheats, and that their behaviour was put on in order to deceive their converts.

In the end, there can be no certainty, once this question has been raised. Just as all the apparent facts that the earth is more or less spherical can be dismissed by flat-earthers (the photographs are fakes; the people who claim to have sailed round the world are liars; it is all a conspiracy), so the evidence for genuine care and affection can be rejected as clever acting by people who are essentially self-centred and only concerned about themselves.

The cost of cynicism

Moreover, those who want to persuade us that we have been deceived have an advantage over those who try to assure us that we are the receivers of genuine affection. There is, in most of us, a reluctance to accept love, and a pride that finds other people's concern for us humiliating and to be resented. We are easy targets for cynicism, and will happily settle for a view of the world that includes the attitude, 'Trust nobody; everybody is only out for what they can get.'

The only defence against this is to see that it is potentially unlimited in its scope: if it were true, there would be no such thing as love, and there would be no way of recognizing it if there were. The thoroughgoing cynic is irrefutable. But at what cost? At the cost of isolation, suspicion, inability to co-operate with others, withdrawal of all faith in everyone. If you know them by their fruits, then the consequences of universal cynicism show it to be false; no one could survive, if it were true.

This letter to the Thessalonians is an attempt to pull its readers back from the edge. They are looking into an abyss, in which nothing can be recognized for what it is. But everything is perceived as an evil parody of the genuine thing: concern for others is seen as flattery; good works are seen as a performance that seeks praise; kindness is a cover for greed; gentleness is a trick; love is self-seeking. The temptation to give in to this is powerful. But if we do give in to it, we are finished, because nothing can reach us to save us from its toils.

In its place there must be the humility that will accept the genuineness of other people's love for us, the freedom to believe that we are approved of, the power to license others to show us affection and to praise us for what we do.

PRAYER

Save me from suspicion and cynicism.
Teach me to accept kindness and praise.
Give me the humility that can receive love.

INVITED *to* RULE *the* WORLD

Again the Thessalonians must recall the facts. How perverse of them to listen to people who say that Paul and his fellow-preachers are deceitful and defrauding their converts! Can they not remember how the visitors would not accept anything without paying in return? They worked night and day to meet the cost of board and lodging.

The subject will come up again, and notice in particular 1 Corinthians 9:5f.: 'Do we not have the right to be accompanied by a believing wife, as do other apostles and the brothers of the Lord and Cephas? Or is it only Barnabas and I who have no right to refrain from working for a living?' People in Corinth argued that Paul was not an apostle because he did not accept expenses, whereas the Jerusalem missionaries did and claimed the authority of Jesus for doing so (1 Corinthians 9:14). It may be, therefore, that those who are causing trouble for Paul and his colleagues in Thessalonica have also come from Jerusalem.

What Paul and his companions had been doing was nothing that could possibly be interpreted as dishonest. They were working to prepare the faithful in Thessalonica for the future. God had invited the Thessalonians to share his own kingdom and glory—that is, he had offered them positions of authority in the coming new age. Psalm 8 would then be fulfilled:

> You have made them a little lower than God,
> and crowned them with glory and honour.
> You have given them dominion over the works of your hands;
> you have put all things under their feet (vv. 5, 6).

This is also what is promised in the beatitudes in Matthew 5:3 and 5. 'Theirs is the kingdom of heaven' is parallel to 'They will inherit the earth'; put together, the meaning is that the blessed will share with God in ruling the earth.

Sharing in the kingdom

The believers are waiting to share in the kingdom, the power and the glory of God; to rule with him, to have some part of his power and some of the glory that is his. Their present life is preparation for future rulership, just as a father might prepare his children to join the family firm when they are grown up, and take up positions of authority in it. They must learn how to be managers; in the case of the Thessalonians, how to be like God and do what God does.

The prospect is daunting to most people. The ideal that is most commonly sought is to lay down authority as we get older and leave decision-making to those who are younger. But it may be that what appeals to us in the West today is not what was longed for in the first century under the Roman Empire. And it may be that what God thinks is different from what we think. Perhaps the age to come should be thought of not as the absence of activity, but as an increase of it—a fuller life, with more to do, rather than an endless sabbath, without work and labour. Certainly no one can have any clear ideas about what the future will be, except that it will be better than the present, and that it will be totally absorbing and completely perfect. Romans 8:32 could be translated: 'He who did not withhold his own Son, but gave him up for all of us, will he not with him give us the universe also?' There is no limit to the generosity of God. This was one of Paul's characteristic insights.

PRAYER

What you have prepared for us passes our understanding.
Sustain our hope of glory.
Let us never doubt your goodness.

The WORD of GOD

There is so much suspicion and uncertainty around in Thessalonica that Paul repeats what he had said in 1:2f.—his thanksgiving to God for the Thessalonians is unceasing. He has no doubt that they are members of the church that is in God and in Christ. The trouble-makers would like them to feel insecure, as though they were not fully in God's grace; then the Thessalonians would listen to them, instead of listening to Paul. He is therefore reassuring them of their genuine-ness as the church in God, by telling them of his uninterrupted thanksgiving. (He uses a word which means literally 'uninterrupted' three times in this letter: 1:2f., here, and at 5:17 where he instructs them to pray without ceasing.)

They became a church that is in God, through the preaching and hearing of the gospel. That was when God called them—invited them into his family. The gospel Paul preached was God's word, and the Thessalonians recognized it as such.

They might not have done so. Paul himself sometimes refers to it as 'my gospel' (Romans 2:16) or 'our gospel' (2 Corinthians 4:3 and 1 Thessalonians 1:5), meaning the way that I and my colleagues pro-claim Christ, which was different from the way others presented the good news. Even so, the Thessalonians were able to distinguish what was said from merely human ideas, and hear the word of God through what was said by human agents.

God's word was powerful; through it he created the heavens and the earth. It accomplished his will, and did not return to him empty; it succeeded in the purpose for which it was sent (Isaiah 55:10f.). By means of Paul's preaching, God's word created the church of the Thessalonians; that was why Paul gave thanks to God for them. It was this word of God that made them embark on their 'work of faith and labour of love and steadfastness of hope in our Lord Jesus Christ' (1:3).

Always remember

Paul is saying to his readers: remember what happened. Remember how it began with the first preaching of the good news in your city. You responded to that preaching in a particular way; you accepted it as a message from God. Do not listen to people who say that those who preached on that day are deceivers, or that they are inferior to other preachers (themselves, for example). What happened, happened because God did something to you, no matter what agents he used for this purpose. Whether Paul and his partners were good men or bad men is entirely irrelevant to the fact that you heard God's word. God can use anybody. What matters is what he does. That he did things to you, you cannot doubt.

All the encouragement that we need to continue in faith is available; it is stored up in our memories, and is there, waiting to be called to mind. Present doubt must not be allowed to distract good memories of the mercy of God towards us in the past. The temptation is to rewrite our autobiographies, omitting what we knew and believed of the goodness of God and his grace at a time when we had greater clarity and conviction. The Thessalonians are doing this, only a few months after it had all happened. How much easier to do it over a span of years, decades.

Paul will write, later, about growing up and finishing with childish things (1 Corinthians 13:11); but not everything that happened in the past comes within this category. There was genuine insight then, and there was authentic response to it. Wholesale disparagement would be a mistake.

PRAYER

Thank you for the power of memory.
Thank you for your goodness in the past.
Thank you for your continuing work in us.

The NEED for STEADFASTNESS

Paul said in the previous verse (v. 13) that the Thessalonians had been able to distinguish the word of God from the word of men; now he gives us the evidence that this is what has happened. The willingness of the Thessalonians to endure persecution shows that their faith was in God, and that God was at work in them.

The three verses of this paragraph (2:14–16) have been the subject of a great deal of study and discussion. It has been said that they exhibit an anti-Jewish point of view that contrasts with what Paul says about the Jews in Romans 9—11. Some writers have argued that this passage in 1 Thessalonians is not by Paul, but that it is an insertion put in by a later writer.

The passage says that the Jews in Judea persecuted the members of the churches in Judea, that they killed the Old Testament prophets and Jesus, that they drove out Paul and his companions, and that they are disapproved of by God. They try to stop Paul and others from preaching to the Gentiles. The Jews have fulfilled their destiny as opponents of God, and his punishment has come upon them—Paul doesn't say how.

We can be fairly certain that Paul knew that believers in Thessalonica were being persecuted for their faith (compare above: 1:3, steadfastness; and 1:6, persecution), just as believers in Judea had also been persecuted. In both cases the persecutors were Jews. But God will bring all this to an end when Christ returns for the final judgment. Then there will be the wrath of God for some, and deliverance from the wrath for others (1:10).

It may be that Paul was not absolutely certain who was causing the trouble in Thessalonica. Timothy had been sent to encourage them (3:1f.) and had returned (3:6). He could tell Paul about the faith of the Thessalonians but perhaps he could not explain where the trouble had come from. It may be that he reported that the opponents of Paul in Thessalonica were pressing the believers to adopt Jewish practices, as Paul's opponents in Galatia were also to do—to keep the Jewish calendar and accept circumcision. Paul seems to associate the troublemakers in Thessalonica with Jews, but to say no more than that. Hence our difficulty in understanding who they were.

Judgment to come

What is certain, however, is that Paul believed that he and everybody else lived in a world that belonged to God and that God would soon show his hand in judgment. He had provided the way of salvation through Jesus. It was open to all to accept God's offer, whether they were Jews or Gentiles; that distinction was now out of date. For one group (whether Jews or Gentiles) to attempt to stop the other group from hearing the good news was to resist God. It was to live in the past and to fail to appreciate what was new.

This is always the problem: to fail to see what has happened; to fail to see that we live in a changed world. Time is irreversible and God has made changes through Christ. Paul's opponents were always 'religious' people whose religion was out of date. It stopped them from accepting the freedom that God had given them.

PRAYER

Make us see what you want us to see.
Stop us from restricting the freedom of others.
Give us the steadfastness of hope.

PAUL'S INTEREST *in the* THESSALONIANS

A new major section of the letter begins at this point. Previously Paul has been reminding the Thessalonians of what they already knew, namely the time when he and the other preachers were with him in Thessalonica. Now, however, he begins to tell them what they may not have known: what happened after they left Thessalonica.

The account of this in Acts states that they left at night, smuggled out of Thessalonica because of persecution caused by local Jews who became jealous (Acts 17:5–10). No doubt this was fuel for those who wanted to argue that Paul and Silvanus and Timothy were frauds: they stayed only so long as they could make something out of their converts, but as soon as there was trouble they were off elsewhere, to repeat the whole process over again.

Three points are made in reply: first, they all longed to be back in Thessalonica (v. 17); second, they all determined to return, Paul himself more than once, but they were thwarted (v. 18); and third, it was in the interest of the missionaries that the Thessalonian church should flourish (vv. 19–20).

In verse 17, Paul uses a word that describes children whose parents have died—literally: 'orphanized'. The metaphor is upside-down since it is the Thessalonians who have lost their father, rather than Paul. The Thessalonians are orphans, not Paul. Perhaps the inappropriateness of the word, taken literally, adds to the force of what Paul is saying: we are desolate without you.

It was, he says in verse 18, Satan who blocked their way. The opposition is described in personal terms, thus including ideas of skill, malice, hatred and enmity that we associate with people, rather than by the use of impersonal expressions such as sickness, poverty, other matters taking priority, absence of transport and so on. The advantage of this personal language is that it does not underestimate the power and cunning of what we are up against. It is difficult to find any other way of saying what needs to be said about the perilousness of our situation.

Verses 19 and 20 suggest that it would be to the permanent, eternal disadvantage of the missionaries, were the Thessalonian church to collapse. God will reward everyone according to his work. Paul will develop this idea in 1 Corinthians 3:10–15. The Day of the Lord will be like a fire that tests material: good material will survive; poor material will be destroyed. The builder who has used poor material will not be rewarded.

In these verses Paul uses a different metaphor: the coming of the Lord Jesus on the last day will be like the reward ceremony at the games, when winners are crowned. The value of the crown will be in proportion to the work done. In this sense the Thessalonian church is Paul's crown. It is in his interest, therefore, that it should still exist when the Lord comes in judgment.

We are embarrassed by talk of rewards and surprised that Paul should use it. But it was not always so. In the sixteenth century, an archbishop of Canterbury could still compose a prayer in which it was asked that God's people, plenteously bringing forth the fruit of good works, might be plenteously rewarded by God. There is a simplicity, innocence and straightforwardness about the idea of rewards. It is a mistake to think we can do without it.

PRAYER

You will give everyone their due reward.
Thank you for this promise.
Purify our works.

FELLOW WORKERS

Paul continues to tell the Thessalonians what happened after he left their city so suddenly. He was desperate to know how the church continued. Did they abandon faith because of persecution? He had told them that there would be trouble. It was part of God's plan: if we suffer with Christ, it is so that we may also be glorified with him (Romans 8:17).

He sent Timothy from Athens back to Thessalonica to find out how they fared. Paul himself (and Silvanus) preferred to be alone in Athens, in order to know about the Thessalonians, such was his concern for them.

Notice how he refers here again (cf. 2:18) to Satan, now as the tempter. The existence of the church is threatened by a personal, evil force, working through those who are causing trouble in Thessalonica.

But just as Satan has his agents, through whom he opposes God's will, so too God has agents through whom he works his will. Timothy is a fellow-believer (a brother) and also a co-worker in preaching the gospel. The Greek manuscripts and other early witnesses to the text of the letter differ from one another at this point. What Paul probably wrote was 'a fellow-worker with God' (as the REB translates it); but those who copied the letter found this too surprising a thing to say— that a human being could be thought of as somebody who worked with God. It seemed to claim too much, to be putting a creature on the same level as the Creator. They changed it to 'servant of God', or in some instances simply omitted the word altogether.

Paul's understanding of this becomes clear when he is writing to the Corinthians. He is comparing his ministry with that of those who have gone out from Jerusalem, and he says: I worked harder than any of them. But immediately he explains how this came about: '…though it was not I, but the grace of God that is with me' (1 Corinthians 15:10). The second sentence does not negate the first: God's grace works in and with and through those whom he inspires. It does not destroy the agent, but enables and fulfils. It raises the created person to a new level and status, which Paul describes with the term 'fellow-worker with God'.

Labouring for the gospel

Paul had spent time building up the church in Thessalonica, and he did not want this work to be wasted, as it would be if the trouble-makers had their way. He refers to what he did in Thessalonica as 'labour' (v. 5)—the word suggests toil, strife, trouble, difficulty. It emphasizes the hardness of the work, more than any other aspect of it.

As Paul sees it, this was a characteristic feature of the way that God was dealing with the world in those last days. He had handed over the proclamation of the good news to human beings. He had not written the gospel on tablets of stone, but involved agents such as Paul and Timothy to preach and teach. Jesus, unlike Moses, had written nothing. When Paul contrasts 'the letter' with 'the Spirit' (2 Corinthians 3:6) he is drawing attention to the difference between the old covenant and the new; to the impersonal method of the Law and the personal method of the gospel.

Paul had addressed the congregation in Thessalonica as 'the church in God'; those who bring the gospel and sustain faith and build up the community are likewise only to be understood in the closest proximity to God—working with him, because of God's grace that is with them.

PRAYER

Thank you for your fellow-workers.
Thank you for using us in your work.
Thank you for involvement in your purposes.

You Are Our Life

The climax of the account of what happened between Paul and the church in Thessalonica is the return of Timothy to Paul. (The letter suggests that the apostle still was in Athens, or at least, says nothing to the contrary; in Acts, it is said that Timothy joined Paul in Corinth and that Silas, that is Silvanus, came with him—Acts 18:5.)

Paul's anxieties are now over: the Thessalonians have not turned against him, but hope to see him again. Their faith has not been destroyed by the devil. Paul prays that he may return to Thessalonica to see them again, and to help to build them up in their faith. There are things that they lack and that he can give them. He will start to do this in the remaining part of this letter.

What is remarkable here is the closeness that exists between the apostle and his converts. He has already spoken of them in terms of a nurse and her own children (2:7), a father and his children (2:11), brothers and sisters (1:4; 2:9, 17; 3:7), his hope and joy, his crown on the last day (2:19f.). Now, he says that they are his 'life': 'We now live, if you continue to stand firm in the Lord' (v. 8). There is no more that he could say. To say to someone, 'You are my life' is to tell them that they are the necessary and essential condition for our own existence.

Paul will reflect on this, when he is writing to the Corinthians in the following years. He will compare the relationship between the believers to that between the parts of a body: 'If one member suffers, all suffer together with it; if one member is honoured, all rejoice together with it' (1 Corinthians 12:26).

He must have been an extraordinarily affectionate person, warm-hearted, loving and completely concerned about other people—not, as some people have thought, harsh and strict. He was the opposite of those who are cold, withdrawn, concerned only about themselves and nothing else. The Thessalonians are only one of his many foundations, and the letters that have been preserved in the New Testament are, presumably, only a selection from a larger number that he wrote. Nevertheless, he writes to them here as though he had no other churches to think about. They are at this moment the only people that matter. He gives himself to them completely and he needs good news of them, as if that were all that mattered.

Caring for one another

We need not be apostles to experience this depth of love. All members of the body can have the same care for one another (1 Corinthians 12:25). Not only can, but should. Christianity is not an individualistic religion, but social, communal, expressing itself in organisms that have a common life. The only way in which Paul can have known this must have been through experience of his relationships with the churches he founded. But he believed that this was how it should be for all the believers. There was one common life for all who were in the body of Christ. Paul organized the collection of money in churches in Macedonia and Achaia, to be taken to churches in Judea, because believers who lived either in Greece or Palestine had one shared life, and this had to be expressed in practical terms.

The warmth with which Paul writes about his joy at the good news that Timothy has brought to him so recently reminds us that we are members of a group that meets in a place but is 'in' God the Father and in Jesus Christ. Detached and isolated Christians are an impossibility—a contradiction.

PRAYER

Thank you for my brothers and sisters in Christ.
Thank you for the care that they have shown for me.
Do not let me cut myself off from them.

PAUL'S FIRST PRAYER

Paul has given accounts of his prayer for the Thessalonians already (1:2ff. and 2:13ff.), but now he writes out, in the letter, what it is that he is praying, using verbs in the form that expresses a wish (see also 5:23 and 2 Thessalonians 2:16, 17; 3:5, 16). The present passage in 1 Thessalonians is therefore the earlier example of a Christian written prayer that has come down to us in its original language.

The first feature to note (and it is very remarkable in a movement that began entirely among Jews, and in a letter written by a man who had been brought up as a strict Jew) is that Jesus is associated with God, in such a way that the prayer is addressed to both of them. The lordship of Jesus places him in the position of being able to hear our prayers and act in response to them. This is what it means to say that he 'sits at God's right hand'.

The first petition is that God and Jesus may make it possible for Paul (and Silvanus and Timothy) to return to Thessalonica. Satan had blocked their way (2:18), but God and Jesus could remove him; this is why the return to Thessalonica is the subject of prayer.

The second petition is for the increase of their love, both towards other members of the church and towards everyone else as well. Paul distinguishes between the church and those outside, but prays that both may be loved.

The third and final petition is for the Thessalonians on the day when Jesus returns, with all his holy ones—the departed members of the church, or the angels, or both. Paul will say more about this in the remaining part of this letter (e.g. 4:15–18).

Standing in God's favour

Both here and in the other direct prayer in this letter (5:23), Paul prays for God's approval of his converts at the coming of Christ and the last judgment. His desire is that nothing may happen to them, between now and the end of this age, to remove them from the favour of God in which they stand.

When he writes to the Corinthians, he quotes an earlier Christian prayer that has survived in Aramaic, even in the Greek-speaking church to which he is writing: *Marana tha*, 'Our Lord, come!' (1

Corinthians 16:21) And even older than that will have been the prayer of Jesus, reported both by Matthew (6:9–13) and Luke (11:2–4), of which the first petitions were for God to act by beginning to rule and accomplish his will, both in heaven and on earth; while the latter part of the prayer was for inclusion in the new age, and final deliverance from the evil one (in Matthew's version).

This way of praying, for the end of the present world order and the beginning of the new age, is in tune with the instruction that Matthew records in the Sermon on the Mount: 'Set your mind on God's kingdom and his justice before everything else, and all the rest will come to you as well' (6:33, REB).

PRAYER

You have made us, redeemed us and sanctified us.
You know what you will do with us.
Do your will.

YOUR SANCTIFICATION

The second main part of the letter begins here. In the first section there was thanksgiving for the church in Thessalonica and prayer for it; now Paul turns to instruction, reminding them of what he had said when he was present, and encouraging them to follow the teaching he shared with them.

As he has said already, they are the church in God because God has chosen them and called them; he is sustaining them through all the troubles that have come upon them, and he will keep them in his favour in the coming judgment and welcome them into the age to come. They belong to God now, and God's will is that they shall always be his property. This is what he means by 'sanctification'—belonging to God.

As we would expect from this, it follows that certain kinds of action are important for those who believe that God has done these things for them. Already Paul has prayed that they may abound in love for one another and for all (3:12); anything unloving is therefore to be avoided. Paul, a Jew, believes non-Jewish sexual practices to be contrary to the will of God. So the first instruction on how to continue in the way of sanctification is to abstain from fornication—a word that covers various sorts of sexual activity outside marriage.

It is not an accident that the oldest piece of Christian writing should contain, as the first instruction to its Christian recipients, the command to abstain from fornication. There was scarcely any area of life in which the customs of Jews differed more markedly from the accepted practices of Gentiles than in this matter. A Gentile becoming a Christian would find this the first and perhaps the hardest rule to keep: no sexual activity outside marriage.

Avoiding abuse

There is a well-known problem of translation in verse 4. The NRSV text has: 'That each of you know how to control your own body in holiness and honour'; and the REB agrees with this: 'Each one of you must learn to gain mastery over his body, to hallow and honour it.' But the NRSV margin has: 'That each one of you know how to take a wife for himself in holiness and honour.' Paul used a word that meant 'a vessel', and could be used both of one's body and of one's wife. Whichever it is that he means, the main point is clear: in sex, we have a problem and we must find out how to cope with it. Paul is against abuse of other people or of ourselves. What he understands by fornication is sin against other people, failure to love, exploitation of others.

This, he believes, is not God's will; it is not sanctification, not love for one another and for all. And God punishes it. Paul is not, he believes, expressing merely his own opinion, but God's instructions; and God has provided help for us to keep his rules, by giving us his Holy Spirit. The situation, Paul believes, is that there is help to do what is for many the most difficult thing.

It is noticeable how unspecific Paul is, in this passage. He does not list activities that are prohibited, but he writes in general terms, and gives two words that are guidelines for action: avoid exploitation; practise love. Many of the problems that would be likely to arise in Thessalonica could be dealt with by means of these two considerations.

PRAYER

Thank you for making me your property.
Thank you for calling me to be holy.
Thank you for the gift of your Spirit.

PHILADELPHIA

The Greek word for 'love of the brothers' is *philadelphia*, a word that was not much used in earlier Greek literature, where it referred mainly to love of those who were literally blood brothers and sisters. Christians used it in the figurative sense of love for the other members of the church. The first part of the word, *phil-*, means to love, as in Europhile, philanthropist, etc. The other part of the word is from *adelpho*, giving *adelphos*—'brother'—and *adelpha*—'sister'. (Hence the NRSV translation 'brothers and sisters', throughout the New Testament.) 'Brother' was used as a technical term in the early years of the Christian movement, to mean a fellow believer, before the word 'Christian' was invented (Acts 11:26). Although some modern translations of the New Testament use the word 'Christian' frequently, in Greek it comes only three times in the whole New Testament, at Acts 11:26, 26:28 and 1 Peter 4:16. Both Acts and 1 Peter are probably fairly late writings, from the end of the first century or the beginning of the second.

Philadelphia therefore refers to love for other members of the churches, while *agape*, another word that means 'love', can be used for love of anyone, believer or not. Paul seems to have accepted that there would be a difference between what was called for in our relationships within the church and what was our duty to everybody. He distinguishes between love for one another and love for all (3:12). Both must be practised but they are different from each other. He makes the same point in his letter to the Galatians: 'Let us work for the good of all, and especially for those of the family of faith' (Galatians 6:10).

The Thessalonians, he says, do love the other members of the churches throughout Macedonia, in the towns and cities where groups of believers are meeting. They only need encouragement to do this more and more. He will write to the Romans, 'Owe no one anything, except to love one another' (Romans 13:8). The obligations of love are never completely fulfilled; see 1 Corinthians 13 for its limitlessness.

Living quietly

There is, however, a hint here of something amiss in the Thessalonian church and it is uncertain what exactly was going on. They are to make it their ambition to live quietly (v. 11)—a paradox: usually ambitious people do not live quietly—and to continue to work in order to earn a living (following Paul's instructions and example). In this way outsiders (i.e. those who are not members of the church) will respect them, and the believers will not need the support of unbelievers. Paul will return to this in 2 Thessalonians 3:6–15.

If the troublemakers in Thessalonica are people from Jerusalem who teach a different version of Christianity from Paul's, then it may be that they were putting into practice the Lord's teaching, 'Labourers deserve their food' (Matthew 10:10). Those for whom Matthew's Gospel was written will have thought of themselves as the hungry, thirsty, strangers, naked, sick and prisoners—the brothers and sisters of the King, who provided the unbelievers with opportunities for ministering to Christ, by serving them (see Matthew 25:31ff.). They were, in effect, the first Christian mendicants (i.e. beggars), and mendicancy then, as later in the Middle Ages, was not always approved of by other Christians.

Paul was against it. He did not practise it himself, and he forbids the churches he has founded to practise it. It is unbecoming, he says, indecent, improper. He supports his argument by collecting money for the poor saints in Jerusalem—those who have nothing, because of their shared and voluntary poverty.

PRAYER

Deliver us from greed.
Make us generous to everybody.
Help us to see the needs of our fellow believers.

The Dead *in* Christ

We can probably assume from this passage that some of the believers in the church in Thessalonica had died, between Paul's visit there and the time of his writing this letter. Moreover, Paul must have heard that these deaths in the congregation had caused distress among the other members of the church: not only the sorrow that everyone may have at such a time, but also confusion over the promises and expectations that the good news had created.

The message that Paul and his companions brought concerned God's kingdom, the time when he would rule and all his enemies would be brought into subjection to him. But, clearly, death still retained its power. So how was a believer to understand Christ's victory?

Paul had referred to faith, love and hope, at the beginning of this letter (1:3). Hope, according to this reckoning, was one-third of the Christian's equipment (see also 5:8). But to grieve for the dead as if they had no future would be to act as one who had no hope.

The word has now lost much of what it meant to Paul and others who used it at that time. To us, to say that we hope for something to happen more often than not includes the possibility that it may not happen. We say, 'I still hope, even though it seems unlikely.' There was no such uncertainty about hope for the first Christians. For them it was simply looking forward to what would take place, longing for it, and living off it, before it happened. To hope for something was almost the same as to wait for it. Because the Christians are waiting for the resurrection of the dead, they should not grieve for the dead, as though they would not share the life of the world to come with them.

Raised up to glory

How would it happen? Jesus died and God raised him up, never to die again. Those who had been baptized had been united with Jesus, in death (in the water) and resurrection (coming up from the water). The dead were therefore still with Christ, and Christ would bring them with him when he came at the judgment—raising up their bodies to become new bodies, not of flesh and blood, but of spirit and glory.

Those who would still be alive (and Paul assumes that he will be among them, and speaks in the first person, 'we') would then be reunited with the dead in a great meeting in the air, to welcome the coming king of the world. Paul uses an expression that describes the welcome given to an emperor when he visited a city: the citizens marched out to meet him and then led him back into the city in a procession.

Paul did not mean that the future life would be lived 'in the air', or even in heaven, but on the new earth. Heaven was God's dwelling-place; he had given human beings the earth for them to live on; hence the idea of inheriting the earth (Matthew 5:5) and of God's kingdom coming and his will being done, on earth (Matthew 6:10).

Paul will take up the same topic of the resurrection of the dead when he writes to the Corinthians (1 Corinthians 15). He gives a further account of his hope there.

What Christians believed about Jesus, that he had died and been raised to life, gave them all that they needed to know in order to have hope. The final enemy had been overcome, and would eventually be removed completely. It would be a mistake to think that this had not happened and would not take place. It would be wrong to grieve as others did, who had no faith in their future life.

PRAYER

Strengthen our faith.
Deepen our charity.
Give us hope.

By the WORD of the LORD

The problem that the Thessalonians have is the relationship between those who will still be alive and those who will have died, when Christ comes again at the end of this age. Someone in Thessalonica must have said that those who were still alive at the end would have some advantage over those who had died before Christ came, and thus, perhaps, that they would never be reunited with their friends.

Paul is saying that this will not be so. It will be no advantage to have survived until the last day, and there will be no separation of the living from the dead. Believers who have died will be raised before Christ comes, and those who are still alive will meet Christ together with those who have died; there will be no difference, as far as meeting Christ is concerned, between being still alive and having previously died. To be in Christ is more important than anything else, even death, because Jesus died and lives.

Paul says that the source of what he says here is 'the word of the Lord' (NSRV; 'a word from the Lord', REB). It is uncertain exactly what he means by this. It may be a saying of Jesus from the time before the crucifixion (if so, it is not found in any of the four gospels in exactly this form), or it may be a saying of Jesus from the time after the resurrection; or, thirdly, an utterance of a Christian prophet, speaking in the name of Jesus. Notice here how Paul will say, further on in this letter, 'Do not despise the words of prophets' (5:20).

Paul refers to the words of Jesus surprisingly infrequently in his letters (see, for example, 1 Corinthians 9:14; 11:23). It is generally taken for granted that when Christians are faced with a divisive issue and want to overcome their disagreements, the first question to ask is, 'Did Jesus say anthing that helps us to solve our problem?' But that was not how it was with Paul.

Saviour Jesus

Paul believed in Jesus as the saviour, who by his death and resurrection had delivered the world from the consequence of sin; Jesus had, moreover, given his Spirit to those who believed the good news, and through this Spirit they would be able to share the mind of Christ and know his will (1 Corinthians 2:16; 7:40).

To Paul (and to many others in the past—the majority, in fact) Jesus was the saviour rather than the teacher; what he did was more important than what he said. It is only the two evangelists, Matthew and Luke, of all the New Testament writers, who present Jesus as teacher and record his teaching. For the others, he is the redeemer, the deliverer, the reconciler, who saves by deeds, not words.

PRAYER

We believe in the resurrection of the dead.
Thank you for the gift of eternal life.
Thank you for Christ's saving work.

How Long?

Paul introduces this section of his letter with the expression 'Now concerning…', a phrase that he uses again when he is writing to the Corinthians in reply to a letter from them to him (see 1 Corinthians 7:1, 8:1, 12:1, 16:1). It may be, therefore, that Timothy has brought a letter from Thessalonica to Paul with questions to which they wanted his answers and one of these questions will have been, 'How long must we wait before Christ returns, the dead rise, evil is abolished and the new age begins?'

He says that they have no need of further instruction from him on this subject, because there is nothing more to be said than what they know already. The end of waiting will come at a time when the majority least expects it, thinking that it is a time of peace and security. It will take the unbelievers unawares and involve them in destruction.

The Christians of the first century, like some of the contemporary Jews, held various opinions about the future, some of which were strictly mutually exclusive—but this is often the case with such expectations. One view was that there would be signs and warnings of what was to happen first, so that people could fit the present into a longer list of disasters leading up to the return of Christ. (See, for example, Mark 13 and the parallels in Matthew 24 and Luke 21, and the Revelation to John.) Another view was that the moment would come as a surprise, without warning. If you thought things were getting worse, you recalled the programme; if you thought nothing seemed to be happening, you remembered that it would be as unexpected as a thief in the night. It would be soon, but no one knew how soon. You had to be ready all the time.

Belonging to the day

Paul here uses the expression 'The day of the Lord', an Old Testament technical term for God's final future age (see, for example, Amos 5:18). The opposite of day is night, but believers were not in the night or in the dark. Their faith made them aware already of what was to happen. They belonged to the day, before it arrived, and that was why they lived the life of the age to come in advance of its coming— awake, aware and sober.

Faith, love and hope (cf. 1:2f.) are the armour that we need to fight off the devil's attacks (cf. Isaiah 59:17 for a similar idea). Faith is trusting God who raised Jesus from the dead for our justification; love sustains us in our relationship with him and with one another; hope makes it possible to draw on the future in the present, and the future is the time of salvation, nearer now than when we became believers (Romans 13:11).

The alternatives are salvation or wrath (i.e. the wrath of God, destruction—see verse 3), the right hand or the left hand of God (Matthew 25:31–33). Faith is accepting the astounding good news that Jesus has rescued us from the wrath that is coming (1:10) by his death and resurrection. He died for us, Paul says. It does not matter whether, like some of the Thessalonians, we die before he comes (4:13) or whether we are still living when it happens. We shall be with the one who died and is alive—as we already are.

Christian encouragement and the building of the church depended on reflection on this good news. The death and resurrection of Jesus together form an act of rescue that is already effective and will continue to be effective, bringing us into the new age and informing us now of our blessedness in the time to come.

PRAYER

Thank you for giving us so much that joy can be unending.
Thank you for what has been done for us.
Let us receive encouragement and give it to others.

RESPECT YOUR LEADERS

As far as we know, Jesus had not laid down any regulations for the organization of his followers in the future. He did not appoint people to the offices of bishop, presbyter or deacon or use those titles in the way that they were to be used later. There is no church order that can be said to have the authority of Jesus, by words he spoke either before the crucifixion or in the days immediately after, as has sometimes been asserted.

What emerged came out of the experience of groups of followers and converts in the years between AD30 and AD100 or so, and probably happened in different places at different rates of development.

Here in the earliest Christian writing that has survived, we have evidence of a community that is being instructed by the apostle who founded it to respect certain of their members who perform functions that can be grouped under the general heading of 'leadership'. Paul does not use titles here. He does not call them presbyters or any such title, but refers to them by means of verbs that describe their activities: 'those who labour among you, and have charge of you in the Lord and admonish you'. Such people, Paul says, must be held in the highest esteem for what they do. He adds without any conjunction, 'Be at peace among yourselves'; implying perhaps that if they respect and esteem their leaders the consequence will be peace in the church. We might say that the purpose of what is sometimes referred to as Holy Orders is to produce good order.

The need for leadership

Any association of people, however small in numbers and however informal in its procedures and business, has to have leadership of some sort, otherwise no one will know where to meet, or when. And if money is involved, someone will have to take responsibility for it; if the meetings are to avoid disorder, someone must preside and people must agree on the process of choosing such a chairman.

Paul's authentic letters provide very little evidence for the use of titles in the churches he founded. There is one reference to 'bishops and deacons' (NRSV margin: or 'overseers and helpers') in Philippians 1:1 and there is a reference to a woman, Phoebe, a deacon (NRSV margin: or 'minister') of the church at Cenchreae, in Romans 16:1. But this does not mean that there was no organization, no leadership, no structure of authority. There was, and Paul is here exhorting the Thessalonians to respect the people involved, and to love them, because of what they are doing for the church.

'Whoever welcomes you welcomes me,' the Lord was believed to have said (Matthew 10:40). Those who laboured for the Lord in the church should similarly be treated as if they were the Lord himself. The Galatians had welcomed Paul is if he were an angel of God, or Christ himself (Galatians 4:14). The Thessalonians must do so too, to those who give up time and effort to serving the community.

No one could be a beneficiary of Christ, without being a member of one of the communities. Detached and isolated individual believers would be like a detached and separated limb or organ of a body—an impossibility.

PRAYER

Thank you for those who labour for me,
have charge of me and admonish me.
Make me esteem them very highly, in love.
Help me to listen to what they say to me.

GOOD WILL *to* ALL

An unmistakable feature of these nine verses, more obvious in Greek but still clearly present in translation, is the repetition of the word 'all' (and its compound 'always'). They come seven times: be patient with all, do good to all, rejoice always, give thanks in all circumstances, test all things, abstain from all forces of evil.

The Greek word that is used here (*pas/pan*) is the one that gives us the term 'panacea', a remedy for all ills, and (as we have seen) that is exactly what Paul believes his gospel to be. It offers no encouragement to those who are idle (cf. 4:9–12): love of the believers does not permit sponging on them. It reassures those who are faint-hearted: there is a God who cares for his world, even more than we had ever supposed; he did not spare his Son (Romans 8:32). The weak-willed find encouragement in it to start again, whatever their failures had been, because they believe that their justification depends on God and not on themselves. It is a message about God and his doings, so we must be patient with everybody and seek their good, just as God himself does, making no distinctions (Romans 3:27–31).

Paul's gospel makes it possible to rejoice, whatever happens, because it is news about the resurrection of the dead; therefore, however deadly the situation may be, there is life on the other side of destruction. Nothing at all can stop us from praying, specifically from giving thanks; everything that happens, good or bad, is grist to this mill; life comes from one who died, because he died. God has dealt with us through Jesus in such a way that we can be always his eucharistic people, thanking him and rejoicing.

It is the Spirit that makes it possible to hear the gospel, and the Spirit continues to speak in the church through the words of Christian prophets. Attention to what they say calls for discrimination, so test everything, rejecting what is false but retaining what is from God. How shall we know which is which? Paul will provide criteria in a letter that he was to send to the Galatians: love, joy, peace, patience, kindness, generosity, faithfulness, gentleness, and self-control (Galatians 5:22f). The test is whether what the prophet says would produce this 'fruit', if we acted upon it.

Good will to everybody

This is Paul's panacea: instruction for everybody in the church, whatever their situation. There are no exceptions: good will is to be our relationship to everybody. What has to be avoided is the temptation to think ourselves special and therefore exempt from these instructions, as though there could be unusual situations in which they did not apply, or exceptional people for whom excuses could be made (largely by themselves). This is self-deception and it is always more subtle and more common than we suppose. We are more inclined to attribute it to others than to confess it in ourselves.

This paragraph of the letter follows on immediately from the instructions about respecting and esteeming the leaders of the group, and the link between the two subjects is not difficult to see. The reason why we need the help of those who labour among us, have charge of us in the Lord and admonish us, is that we are so blind to our own faults that we cannot see ourselves as others see us, or as we are to God. Self-knowledge is distorted by self-love. The only hope for us is that there will be people who will not be afraid to tell us the truth about ourselves. This is one of the reasons why isolated and detached believers are in such danger. They have no one to tell them when they are deceived about themselves—no one to warn them of logs in their eyes (Matthew 7:1–5).

PRAYER

Stop me from thinking I am exceptional.
Make me accept criticism, reproof, rebuke.
What I need but do not want is humiliation,
in order to learn humility.

PAUL'S FINAL PRAYER & INSTRUCTIONS

Once again, as at 3:11, Paul prays to God for the church at Thessalonica: for its sanctification. He had started the letter with the surprising statement that the church was 'in God' (1:1); now he returns to that belief, and asks that God will complete what still has to be done. As in the earlier prayer, this one too is for the coming of the new age and for all that that will involve. The God of peace will give them peace; the God who is holy will make them holy. This will happen when Christ returns and God's enemies are destroyed.

It was generally expected, by Jews and (therefore) by the first Christians, that life would become more difficult as this age drew to its end. The author of Daniel expressed this in a sequence of metals: gold, sliver, bronze, iron—each less valuable than the one before, each harder (Daniel 2; see also the beasts in Daniel 7, the fourth different from its predecessors, and more dreadful). But they were not to lose heart; they had become members of the church because God had called them. It had not been their decision, but his. They had not invited Paul and his companions to come to Thessalonica and set before them their interesting new ideas. It was all to do with God, God's agents, God's good news. If, then, their entry into the church was through God, and if being in the church was being 'in God', how could they think that he would abandon them before the return of Christ? God can be relied upon. What he has done and does now is the guarantee of what he will do in the future.

Spirit, soul and body

Paul uses here a threefold description of what we are: spirit, soul and body. He more frequently has a twofold distinction, i.e. body and spirit (Romans 8:10). The longer formula is probably used in order to emphasize what God will do, and to express its completeness: he will raise our bodies, glorify our souls, fill our spirits with his Spirit. Nothing will be omitted, in order that we may live the perfect and complete life of the age to come, on the new earth of his creating.

Paul does not suffer from false self-confidence. He knows that he needs God's grace, just as his converts need it. He asks them, therefore, to pray for him, just as he prays for them. Grace creates a sense of mutuality and interdependence.

The command to greet all the members of the church with a holy kiss and to make sure that the letter is read to all of them, together with the description of God as the God of peace, show (once more) that there is trouble in the church and divisions and rivalries among the members. The second letter to the Thessalonians will tell us more, if it was sent soon after the first, and if it describes a situation that was already in its early stages when Paul wrote 1 Thessalonians. It is possible that at this point in his dealings with the Thessalonians, Paul had not yet realized the extent of the divisions in the church and the strength of the opposition to him. But this should not be taken to mean that he would have qualified or even withdrawn what he says here. All the members are to be greeted with a holy kiss. There are no enemies in Christ, only brothers and sisters (2 Thessalonians 3:15, NRSV margin).

PRAYER

Thank you for Paul's letter.
Let me take it to heart.
May the grace of our Lord Jesus Christ be with us.

EN ROUTE

The letter begins with a reference to the steadfastness and faith of the Thessalonians. Other churches are being told about this—how the Thessalonians are meeting persecution and affliction. This is the first topic that is mentioned and it provides us with a clue to understanding the letter as a whole.

Events have moved on since the writing of 1 Thessalonians. We could see then that trouble was brewing, though we could not be sure who was causing it, or what it was about. Now in 2 Thessalonians we can see at least what the disagreement is about. Is the day of the Lord already here (2:2)? Some people in Thessalonica are saying that it is and acting as though it were the time of the final and endless sabbath: they have given up work and are living in idleness (3:6–13).

Work must continue

They have misunderstood God's programme, and their position in it. The day of the Lord is still in the future, so it is not yet the time to abandon work. They should be able to see this from the fact that we are not yet into the time of peace. Peace will come, when Jesus comes; he will bring it. The absence of peace is evidence for the absence (in a sense) of Jesus; that is, it is still the time of waiting and of being persecuted. The present requires us to be faithful and steadfast; we are not yet into the time of seeing and enjoying.

The second letter to the Thessalonians rubs our noses in the fact that the church is *en route* and has not yet arrived. We walk by faith, not by sight (2 Corinthians 5:7). So we should not be surprised by the imperfection of Christian institutions, as though imperfection proved them inauthentic. It is not true that if we were the church of God (and in God, see 1:1) we would be united in faith and love and hope; or that we would all know the truth and there would be no uncertainty or disagreement about what to believe and what to do. Clarity and certainty belong to the future; the present is the time for seeing in a mirror, dimly (1 Corinthians 13:12).

The first four verses of 2 Thessalonians are almost identical to the first three verses of 1 Thessalonians. There are the same three names

(Paul, Silvanus and Timothy), the same description of the church (in God the Father [or our Father] and the Lord Jesus Christ). There is the same thanksgiving for faith, love and hope (or steadfastness, which is the way in which hope shows itself; see 1 Thessalonians 1:3). The new element here in 2 Thessalonians is the emphasis on the third member of the triad: steadfastness. That is what is called for in a time like the present, a time of persecution and affliction.

As far as we can see from this letter, the trouble in Thessalonica has come from within the fellowship, and not from the synagogue or from those in authority in the civil administration. The conflict is within the church; the troublemakers are brothers, believers (3:15, NRSV margin; REB has 'one of the family'). The church *en route* is not yet perfect (1 Thessalonians 3:10).

It is a mistake to expect it to be perfect, and to be overwhelmed with despair when it is evident that it is not. It is equally a mistake to expect ourselves to be perfect and to be excessively despondent when it is apparent that we are not. We must long for the future, both for the church and for ourselves, when everything will be different—when we have arrived. Meanwhile, there is endurance, steadfastness and hope.

PRAYER

Stop us from clutching at false straws.
Make us accept the facts.
Sustain our hope.

TRUST GOD

Belief in a future judgment of the living and the dead—which we find at the end of the book of Daniel, for example (some to everlasting life, and some to shame and everlasting contempt, Daniel 12:2)—provides those who are being persecuted with hope for the future. God will reverse the present situation. Those who are last now will be first then, and those who are first now will be last then. The mighty will be put down and the meek exalted.

The fact that the persecuted continue to be steadfast in faith is evidence that God, who gives faith, is righteous and will deal justly with them in the future. He can be trusted.

Present suffering has a positive purpose. It is intended to make the sufferers worthy of the kingdom of God; that is, of the time after the coming of Jesus, who will put down all God's enemies, so that God will be all in all (1 Corinthians 15:20–28).

There will be no doubt about it, when this has taken place, because all opposition to God will be abolished, totally and for ever. So those who say that the day of the Lord is already here cannot have understood what that means. God has not settled for something less than perfection and the completion of his purposes. We shall not always be as we are now, nor will the world always be as it is. Thank goodness!

The reference to the fire, the vengeance, the punishment, the eternal destruction and separation from the presence of the Lord, and from the glory of his might, may all seem to us crude and uncaring. This is an aspect of traditional Christianity that is frequently found to be unpopular nowadays. It is also not prominent elsewhere in Paul's surviving letters. The purpose of it here is not to inform us about the future, and certainly not to give us grounds for gloating over the fate of those who do not believe, but to deal with one specific question: are we, or are we not, living in the kingdom of God here and now? This cannot be the end; there must be more than this. We want there to be more; we want perfection. We shall have it.

We have hope

The reference to flaming fire gives us hope. Fire purifies: gold and silver are put into the fire to destroy whatever is impure in them. The day of the Lord will be like fire, and only good work will survive it (1 Corinthians 3:10–15). We do not want it to be otherwise.

The fact that time has not yet run out also gives us hope; we are not yet at the point when it will stop. There is still time in which to be made perfect.

Believers have every reason to trust God. What he has begun in them he will complete. He will purify us of all that is false and replace it with what is true.

God will do this, so that the name of Jesus may be glorified through those who are his own; people will see that Jesus is the saviour, because they will see those whom he has saved. The grace and favour of God will be seen by everybody.

PRAYER

Thank you for giving us time.
Use it to mend us and make us perfect.
What we have not, give us; what we are not, make us.

I Am Not Worthy

The prayer for the recipients of the letter is that they will be made worthy of God's call. They are believers, because God called them. What he began he will finish (1 Thessalonians 5:24). What is prayed for is therefore what God will do. This is why we can be confident that it will happen.

In English, the word 'worthy' has recently had a bad time. It has come to be used ironically, meaning 'estimable yet somewhat unimaginative, ineffectual or sanctimonious' (*New Shorter Oxford English Dictionary*).

Here, it is used in a totally different sense. The prayer is that the readers may be in harmony with God's plan for them and so be able to do what faith requires them to do. God has a purpose for them: may it be fulfilled.

There is no sense here of merit, or of qualifying by fulfilling certain conditions. Just the opposite. What is prayed for is God's grace and that is freely available through Jesus Christ. This is why he will be glorified by the believers: their salvation on the last day and their acceptance by God into his kingdom will be evidence not of their good works done to qualify them for the age to come, but of his generosity, kindness, goodness. Everyone will see clearly that the faithful are his handiwork and they will praise him for it.

Jesus' name (i.e. reputation) will be glorified. He will be seen to be the one who saves. He glorifies sinners and he is glorified by doing so.

Ezekiel had said that God would act for his own name's sake. He would alter the way people thought about him by saving his people Israel from exile in Babylon, restoring them to their own land and giving them prosperity (Ezekiel 36:22–38).

Caught up in the love of God

If God acts for the sake of his name, we can be all the more sure that he will do so. Ezekiel believed that he had heard good news: 'It is not for your sake, O house of Israel, that I am about to act, but for the sake of my holy name' (36:22). God's motivation lies within himself, so we need have no anxiety that he will fail to do what he says he will do. Or to put it another way: we are caught up in the love of God; made out of nothing, by his love; redeemed by it; and also to be perfected by it. There is one love that carries us through from our beginning to our end.

Worthiness is appropriateness, appropriateness is faith; faith says, I am not worthy, but Christ died for me—therefore I am worthy.

The readers of the letter need someone to pray for them. They cannot be left to get it right for themselves. By themselves, they will make mistakes. That is why they need an intercessor.

PRAYER

Thank you for those who pray for me.
Thank you for Christ who died for me.
Thank you for calling me to your kingdom.

WORK *of* FAITH

As early as New Testament times, there were people who contrasted 'faith' and 'works'. They thought that one was the opposite of the other: if you had faith, then you did not do anything, you had no 'works'. They said that this was how people were saved—by faith, not by works. Works (i.e. deeds) were visible for others to see; faith was a private matter, between the believer and God.

The letter of James exposes this as nonsense. Faith and works, the writer says, are not opposites; neither of them excludes the other. A faith that did not lead on to doing actions would be a dead faith; living faith shows itself in performance (James 2:14–26).

How did it come about that anyone arrived at the idea that there could be something called faith that did not express itself in actions? It seems to have happened through a misunderstanding of the letters of Paul, by people who were not entirely aware of what he meant and of the context in which he wrote his letters.

The contrast between faith and works appears first (as far as we know) in Paul's letter to the Galatians (ch. 3: for example, compare 3:9, where a literal translation would be 'those who are of faith ... faithful Abraham', with the next verse—'all who are of works of law'). Those who are 'of faith' are blessed by God; those who are 'of works of law' are cursed by God. Anyone not knowing the whole background and context might think that Paul was contrasting faith with any kind of activity. But that was not so. He was contrasting faith (which issues in a wide variety of activities) with obedience to the Law in the Old Testament, which also issues in a whole series of activities—circumcision of males, observance of the sabbath and of food laws, and the complete lifestyle of the observant Jew. Paul had no intention of stopping the recipients of his letters from doing good; he exhorted them to perform good works, and he believed that God would reward them according to what they had done.

Therefore, when Paul uses the expression 'work of faith' (here, and in 1 Thessalonians 1:3) he is not putting together two things that he thought were opposites of each other ('work' and 'faith'); rather, he is referring to a new area of activity that has now opened up for the believer. To believe the gospel is to enter a set of relationships that had not existed previously. You joined a family of brothers and sisters, and you now had obligations to them that you had not had before.

Particularly if you had been a Gentile, you turned from idols to worship the living and true God, and to wait for his Son from heaven (1 Thessalonians 1:9f.). This attracted criticism from others (who continued to worship idols), disapproval, ill will and persecution.

Made worthy

Faith involved doing things you had never thought of before, and enduring as you had never had to endure before. The Thessalonian believers might well think that they met these new demands inadequately, that there were gaps between what they knew they should do and what they actually did. If so, they were not to despair. God can make them 'worthy': he can do this by his power to fulfil their resolve to do good—the deeds that spring from faith. God's power works in the direction of his love: he wills the perfection of his creatures, and makes up what is deficient in their minds and in their performance.

There is therefore no need for the believers to be depressed, as they see how short they fall of what they know they should be and do. They can rely on God to fulfil them—to make them perfect. And they can rest assured that this is what Paul is praying for.

PRAYER

Thank you for the good works
that you have prepared for us to accomplish.
Thank you for making room in your purpose for our works.
Thank you for making up our deficiencies.

73 2 THESSALONIANS 2:1–12

The END IS NOT YET

This paragraph is the part of 2 Thessalonians that is best known, and it is probably because of it that the letter has been preserved. It refutes those who say that the day of the Lord is already here, and who also use that belief to justify themselves in adopting a particular lifestyle which is referred to as 'idling' (3:6–15).

There is a similar passage in Mark, the earliest of the four gospels; Jesus addresses the four disciples (whom he had called at the beginning of his ministry) in private, on the Mount of Olives (Mark 13:3–37). It is the only long, continuous speech of Jesus in Mark's book and was clearly of great importance to him and his readers. As in 2 Thessalonians, the theme is that Christ's return to gather the elect (Mark 13:27; cf. 2 Thessalonians 2:1) will be preceded by various disasters, each worse than the one before. Since these had not yet happened, it was a mistake to think that Christ had come, or that the day of the Lord had already dawned. ('Beware that no one leads you astray', Mark 13:5—see also verse 21. Compare 'We beg you … not to be quickly shaken in mind or alarmed…', 2 Thessalonians 2:1, 2.)

The source of this teaching is probably the book of Daniel in the Old Testament, in which the writer sees the events that led up to Antiochus Epiphanes' destruction of the temple in Jerusalem (165BC) as the final days before the coming of the time when *God* would rule on the earth, instead of the four great empires of the Babylonians, Medes, Persians and Greeks (see Daniel 2 and 7).

Both in Mark and in 2 Thessalonians, the argument is that the expected events have not yet happened, therefore the kingdom has not yet come. Things must get even worse before they can get better —infinitely worse, then infinitely better.

There is to be a final Satanic figure, a rebellion against God, and the destruction of this agent of Satan by Christ. (The same sequence of events is also expected in Revelation: the first beast in Revelation 13:1–10 is the Satanic agent and Christ is the rider on the white horse, who makes war with him—Revelation 19:11–21.)

Whatever we make of this kind of thinking, two points are clear. First, it was so specific that it answered anyone who claimed, as the troublemakers did in Thessalonica, that they were already in the age to come, and that the appropriate way of living was to abandon work and live off whatever capital the community had—or, perhaps, become beggars.

Second, apocalyptic expectations such as we have here, and in Mark 13 and the book of Revelation, offer us a way of thinking about life in general that is the opposite of what many people believed towards the end of the nineteenth century and in the early part of the twentieth. Everything would get better, they thought; there would be progress. Advances in knowledge would inevitably guarantee improvements in the way people lived. They expected life to get better; those who lived at the time of the early church expected it to get worse.

The Lord's Prayer comes from the same world of thought as these apocalyptic passages in the New Testament, and the first three petitions are for God to act so as to bring in his new and final age, the kingdom of God. It cannot happen without him, but we have to pray for it to happen.

PRAYER

Hallow your name.
Begin your rule.
Do your will, here and everywhere.

By LETTER, *as* THOUGH *from* US

People are telling the Thessalonians that the day of the Lord is already here; indeed they are saying that Paul has said so. That is to say, they claim the authority of Paul for what they are teaching. Paul is correcting this misunderstanding. One of the ways in which this mistake could have arisen, he says, is through a letter that seemed to be from Paul.

The letter in question may be the first letter to the Thessalonians; and Paul may be saying here, in the second letter, that it was wrong to think that he had meant, in his first letter, to say that the day of the Lord had arrived. All he had meant was that it would come when no one was expecting it (1 Thessalonians 5:1–11).

But there is another possibility that should be mentioned here: it may be that there were letters being passed around in churches at this time, that claimed to be by Paul, but were not in fact written (or dictated) by him. The ending of this second letter could be understood in relation to this: 'I, Paul, write this greeting with my own hand. This is the mark in every letter of mine' (3:17). The recipients of 2 Thessalonians will thus have a way of testing any other letter that comes 'as though from us': has it got Paul's handwriting at the end of it?

Ideas of authorship

This opens up a problem that we today find extraordinarily difficult to understand. Our idea of right and wrong with regard to authorship of writings is different from that of those who lived in the ancient world. It seems that it was accepted that you could write under the name of someone more famous than yourself, and that you could (or should) do this to express the other person's ideas—'this is what so-and-so would have said'.

Some such belief may lie behind the letter of Barnabas (apparently regarded as holy scripture by the scribe of *Codex Sinaiticus*), and by those who attributed their writings to Peter, Philip, Thomas or almost any other prominent figure in the first-century churches.

It is very common to find commentators on the New Testament who think that Paul himself did not write 1 and 2 Timothy, or Titus, but that they are by a disciple of Paul, writing what he believed Paul would have said. As we have seen earlier (Introduction, page 105) some people think that 2 Thessalonians is also by someone other than Paul.

It would be very wrong to use words like 'forgery', 'dishonesty' or 'deceit' of this practice, which seems to have been widespread, among Jews, Greeks and Christians. The treasure (which is the gospel) comes to us in clay jars (2 Corinthians 4:7). God uses people with ideas that may be different from ours.

PRAYER

Thank you for using us.
Help us to distinguish the treasure from the clay.
Lead us into the truth.

The LAWLESS ONE
& the ONE who RESTRAINS

Some further explanation is needed about two figures who are referred to in this paragraph: 'the lawless one', and 'the one who now restrains'. These titles are not used elsewhere in scripture in exactly this form, but the ideas involved appear also in other passages that share this apocalyptic point of view. The lawless one, for example, is almost certainly the same figure as antichrist, mentioned by this title only once in the New Testament: 'As you have heard that antichrist is coming, so now many antichrists have come' (1 John 2:18).

The background and origin of these ideas is the book of Daniel. It seems to have been written in the second century BC at the time when the Greek king, Antiochus IV, ruled over the eastern Mediterranean, including Jerusalem and Judea. His chosen title was Epiphanes, meaning 'manifestation' (of Zeus). He had ordered the desecration of the altar in the temple in Jerusalem, which is described in 1 Maccabees 1 (e.g. v. 59) and referred to in Daniel 11:31.

Once this event had become part of a sacred book (i.e. Daniel) it was recycled as a standard prophecy about the future, hence the reference to it in Mark 13:14 and the parallel in Matthew 24:15. This idea of a ruler claiming divine powers and insisting on being worshipped was almost repeated in AD40 when the Emperor Gaius (Caligula) attempted to have his statue erected in the temple in Jerusalem. For a later prophecy of this expected final manifestation of evil, see Revelation 13:1–10—the beast rising out of the sea.

In the minds of the Hebrews (as in our minds too), major events in history were associated with identifiable individuals: Nebuchadnezzar and the exile, Cyrus and the return from exile, Antiochus Epiphanes and the desecration of the altar, Herod the Great and the rebuilding of the temple. So, too, a final rebellion of the world against God was expected, and the leader of the rebellion, it was thought, would be an individual—'the man of lawlessness' or 'the man of sin' (NRSV margin, 2:3).

Heavenly powers

'The one who now restrains' (2:7, cf. also 2:6) is probably another 'power', perhaps the angelic being who gives authority to the Roman Empire. For a similar idea, see Daniel 10:20f., where there are references to the prince of Persia, the prince of Greece, and 'Michael, your prince'—all principalities and powers in the heavenly places, who watched over 'their' nations (cf. Deuteronomy 32:8–9).

Roman justice and organization is keeping back the final rebellion; Paul will refer to this when he writes to the church in Rome (13:1–7). When the time comes for God's plan to be fulfilled, the one who restrains will be removed, and evil will have its way for the last time.

It is ideas like this that probably lie behind what we say in the second part of the Lord's Prayer: 'Do not bring us to the time of trial, but rescue us from the evil one' (Matthew 6:13). We should not assume that we shall find the future less troublesome than the past; the prayer teaches us to beware of false confidence in our ability to resist temptation.

PRAYER

Give us the humility to ask for help.
Give us the confidence that trusts you to help us.
Save us from despair as things get worse.

GOD'S PLAN *for* EVERYBODY

Twice in this short letter it is said that thanksgiving is imperative: 'We must always give thanks to God for you' (1:3); and again, 'We must always give thanks to God for you, brothers and sisters beloved by the Lord' (2:13). The belief that lies behind these statements of what must be is that God has a plan; that the recipients of the letter are part of this plan; that God intends to do something for them; and that this is to their advantage—it does in fact exceed all their expectations. The readers of the letter must therefore share in the thanksgiving of the writer.

They must see themselves as people who are loved by God. They can be sure that this is so, because they know that faith came to them as a gift from God. They realized that he had chosen them, not they him. He had chosen them for salvation—that is, for an eternal future with God. To prepare them for this, he had given them his own Spirit, to transform them from what they had been, and make them into what they would have to be to live with God. He had dealt with them through the preaching of the gospel by Paul and his companions in Thessalonica, and he would give them a share of the glory which he had given to his Son, Jesus Christ.

The Greek manuscripts, on which we depend for our knowledge of the text of this letter, disagree with one another in verse 13: some of them have an expression that means 'as the first fruits' (so NRSV, and REB margin); others have 'from the beginning' (so REB, and NRSV margin). In Greek, the difference involves only one letter. Whichever was the original, the main point is the same: the choice was God's, not ours; it is not our plan, but his.

Intended for glory

This is certainly so if we think what it is that God has decided to do for us. He intends that we should have the same glory that Jesus now has. However great our hopes for ourselves had been, it is very unlikely that we should ever have entertained such an idea for ourselves, and by ourselves. We might have had more modest expectations of a future existence of some sort, but nothing too excessive or elaborate. God's plan for us goes beyond anything anyone could reasonably contemplate: 'Such good things as pass man's understanding', 'more than we desire or deserve'. This extreme generosity can only be of God. It is beyond the range of our expectations.

The whole idea of glory has been made to seem suspect. Sometimes our elders frowned on us when we expressed childish hopes of success, eminence, wealth and splendour. But that is exactly what we are to have; it would be a mistake not to desire it. What was mistaken was the idea that we had to compete in order to have it ('I'm the king of the castle') and the way we imagined we should achieve it (by conflict: 'Get down you dirty rascal'). We were wrong in both respects: there is enough glory for everyone to have it all; and it will come to us as a gift, earned for us, not by us.

So of course thanksgiving is imperative; there is the 'must' and the 'always' too. It is God we must thank because it is entirely his plan, completely beyond our imagining; and he will not change his mind about us—he will *always* be for us.

PRAYER

Enlarge our expectations of what is in store for us.
Increase our faith in your goodwill towards us.
Deepen our thanks for your undeserved love.

TILL WE HAVE BUILT JERUSALEM

The readers of the letter must stay with what they were taught originally by those who brought the gospel to Thessalonica. They must
stand firm and hold on to the things that were said then. They must
not pay attention to those who are deceiving them into thinking that
the day of the Lord is already here.

God had called them to greater things than anything they had
already received from him. What was still in store for them was more
than their present gifts. So they needed encouragement to hope—to
look forward to a future that they could never imagine because it
would be so good.

Their mistake was to think that the gifts they had received were the
sum total of all that God had in store for them. They had received the
Spirit, and no doubt they could prophesy (1 Thessalonians 5:19f.)
and speak with tongues. We can see how the believers in Corinth val-
ued these gifts excessively, and what Paul said to them (1 Corinthians
12—14).

Greater things to come

God promises far greater things still: a new heaven and a new earth
ruled by God, with his will being done everywhere. This has not yet
happened; to say that it has is to make excessive claims for charis-
matic gifts, instead of believing that the whole of creation is waiting
for its redemption. (See, for example, Romans 8:18–25—the creation
'waits with eager longing for the revealing of the children of God', at
the final judgment.)

As long as Claudius is emperor (AD41–54), or Nero (AD54–68), or
anyone else, it would be wrong to think that God had completed all
that he intended for this world.

It is sometimes said that religion should keep out of politics; but,
for Christians, this is impossible. No government, however good, can
take the place of the direct rule of God. That is why we must always
be critical of the present authorities and always be praying for God to
take their place: 'Thy kingdom come.'

This was the main theme of the book of Daniel, and its influence
on the writers of the New Testament was extensive. World empires, it

was believed, would become progressively more cruel and merciless (gold, silver, bronze, iron and clay, Daniel 2), until God finally intervened and instituted his rule that would never end.

To pray for this to happen was to be committed to its coming and so to work for it. This is why the Thessalonians need to be comforted (i.e. strengthened) in good works. Their labour will not be in vain. God will incorporate their good deeds into the city that will come. They will see that the new Jerusalem has been built by them. People will bring into it the glory and honour of the nations (Revelation 21:26).

PRAYER

Sustain our hope.
Make us long for Jerusalem.
Show us what you want us to do.

PRAYER & STEADFASTNESS

If the day of the Lord had come, as some were saying, there would have been no need to continue to pray. Nor would there have been need for the preaching of the gospel. But it had not come, so the Thessalonians must pray, and in particular they must pray for those who preach the gospel.

The missionaries need the prayers of the church because they are exposed to constant and life-threatening dangers, both obvious (in the form of persecution, imprisonment, beating, etc.) and subtle (i.e. temptations).

The church is militant, here on earth, fighting against evil and unbelieving people. But in this warfare they have the assurance of God's help and they can rely on him and be confident.

There are two elements that can build up the Thessalonians' confidence: one is the love of God and the other is the steadfastness of Christ.

The love of God (i.e. God's love for us) is the root cause of the way things are. He is not simply a God of power and might; if he had been, he would not have needed to involve his creatures in the attainment of his purpose. He is more than simply almighty: his power serves the end of his love; and from this love it follows that he works with his creatures, and empowers them to work with him.

Fellow-workers with God

Prayer is valid because God is love. Instead of acting unilaterally, he gives us scope to pray and waits for this to happen. The delay in bringing in the end leaves us time to pray for it to come. He takes us seriously as his fellow-workers.

Similarly, Christ's steadfastness is another reason for confidence. He chose to die; that was his one act of righteousness (Romans 5:18). Steadfastness includes the idea of endurance, of accepting suffering as the way to something better. This steadfastness is available for those who are in Christ. He will share it with them as they share his suffering now, waiting and longing for the glory that lies in the future.

When Paul writes to the Romans, he will say to them, 'Suffering produces endurance (i.e. steadfastness), and endurance produces character, and character produces hope, and hope does not disappoint us, because God's love has been poured into our hearts' (Romans 5:3–5).

PRAYER

Keep us steadfast in hope.
Remind us of your love for us.
Make us faithful in prayer.

BROTHERS & SISTERS,
PRAY *for* US

Paul asks for the prayers of the members of the church he is writing to, both here and in other letters (2 Corinthians 1:11; 1 Thessalonians 5:25). He does this because he believes that their prayers will be effective: they will make it possible for him to continue to preach the gospel, and they will enable him to survive the destructiveness of the opposition that the preaching provokes. The life of an apostle in the Roman Empire of the first century was not easy; Paul knew this—that was why he asked his readers for their prayers.

Is it possible to continue to believe that praying for other people does them any good? Is life any different for those for whom we pray? Or is praying for other people one of those old religious practices that must be abandoned by the present-day believer—a superstition that has no rational basis?

Good wishes

There is no doubt that we still believe in the value and reality of our good wishes. The proof of this is the popularity and immense variety of greeting cards and the market for them. Expressions of good wishes can be bought to suit all possible occasions. But the question is bound to occur to us: are our good wishes only effective if we inform the person to whom they relate? Does it only work if I send the card to let them know? Or would there be any point in my bearing somebody in mind, even if that person did not know that I was doing so?

To ask people to pray for you, or simply to remember you, at a critical time, is a procedure that may or may not imply faith in the effectiveness of prayer and good wishes. At the least, it expresses your feeling of isolation and your need for support and encouragement. But it may do more than that. We ask for food and drink because we know that such things exist and satisfy our needs. It may be the same with prayer: we ask for it, because we know that it works.

The difficulty with this analogy is that anyone can see that food and drink do satisfy hunger and thirst, and how it is that they do so. There is no mystery about that. But how could praying for somebody do anything for them? By what route will the prayers of the Thessalonians reach Paul when he is hundreds of miles away, and have any influence on him?

The obvious answer is that the route is via Paul's memory: he had asked the Thessalonians for their prayers, and he remembers this from time to time; that is the way that intercession works and is effective.

This is inadequate, as anyone who has asked people to think of them, remember them, pray for them, knows. What happens is that things go better than you had expected; you wonder why, and then remember. You had forgotten that you asked for help, but you recall it, after it has happened. It is not the recollection of asking that is effective; it is the prayers of those who were asked that explain why the situation has turned out better than expected.

Maybe what happens is that we are more or less aware of goodwill or ill will in the places where we are, and those who pray for us add to the good will, just as those who oppose us add to the ill will. Certainly there is no proof, other than what those who requested prayer have in their own experience.

PRAYER

Help me to believe in prayer.
Keep me at it.
Thank you for those who do it.

SELF-DECEPTION

Some members of the church at Thessalonica have come to the conclusion that there is no need for them to work in order to earn a living. They can live off the community. Although it is not said explicitly, the reason they gave for doing this could have been that they believed that the end of the world was near.

In the gospels, when the disciples are sent out on their mission, there are sayings of the Lord commanding them to accept accommodation from those who receive them. (See Mark 6:7−13 and Matthew 10:10: 'The worker deserves his keep', REB. Notice also the description of the church in Jerusalem, in Acts 2:43−47.)

It may be, therefore, that those who were causing the trouble in Thessalonica, like those in Corinth (1 Corinthians 9), used the Lord's command to accept board and lodging without paying for it, and thereby claimed superiority over Paul who did not use this right (1 Corinthians 9:15−18). He worked, so as to avoid being a burden to his converts.

The argument may have gone like this: 'We believe the day of the Lord is already here. Old things have passed away, including work, money, private property, the distinction between mine and thine. It is right that we should be supported by others, as the Lord said.'

There are always those who find work tedious and demeaning. They will be glad of any reason to avoid it, and the (apparently) more religious the reason, the better. Our power to deceive ourselves is almost infinite, and beliefs about God are not immune from being used for this purpose.

There is evidence that the problem did not go away. In a document entitled *The Teaching of the Twelve Apostles*, written perhaps at the end of the first century, instructions are given as to how to distinguish a true prophet from a false prophet. Visiting prophets were entitled to free food and so on, but if one stayed more than two days, he showed that he was a false prophet.

The idlers in the community are also called busybodies, not doing any work. In Greek there is a play on words. J. Moffatt's translation is 'busybodies instead of busy'. This too is an example of self-deception, of not practising what you preach, of telling other people what to do instead of doing what you should yourself. It is the situation of those who have logs of wood in their eyes, but think they can see specks in the eyes of others (Matthew 7:1–5).

Only a fool would claim exemption from the rule that we are blind to our own character, and ignorant about our own motives. We are trapped in almost complete misunderstanding about ourselves, and we need a powerful force to deliver us from it. Notice how, twice over in these ten verses, reference is made to commands in the name of our Lord Jesus Christ (vv. 6 and 12). There is provision in the church for those in authority to declare God's will to us and we would be unwise not to listen to them. There are traditions and customs that protect us from the power of strong personalities who take over communities and enforce their will upon them. We are not left to the mercy of our ignorance and stupidity.

PRAYER

Thank you for the traditions of the church.
Thank you for the insights of others.
Do anything to stop us from deceiving ourselves.

PEACE *in the* CHURCH

The letter ends with instructions on how to deal with members of the church who refuse to obey what the letter says. It is noticeable that what is said here is less severe than what Paul says when he writes to the Galatians. There the troublemakers are anathematized (Galatians 1:8, 9), that is, put under a curse and therefore excluded from the congregation. Here they are to be treated as members of the family (NRSV margin: 'brothers') who must be coaxed by means of persuasion—'sent to Coventry' until they change their minds.

If we take the view that 2 Thessalonians was written soon after 1 Thessalonians, and that those who said that the day of the Lord was already present were Jewish-Christians from Jerusalem, who had come to Thessalonica with (or claiming to have) the authority of James in Jerusalem, and if they were the same people as those who caused trouble in Galatia and elsewhere, then we can see how Paul's instructions to the churches become sharper as the full scale of the situation gradually becomes clearer to him.

In the first letter to the Thessalonians he said, 'Admonish the idlers, encourage the faint-hearted, help the weak, be patient with all of them' (5:14). Here in the second letter he says, 'Have nothing to do with them, so that they may be ashamed. Do not regard them as enemies, but warn them as brothers' (3:14, 15). In Galatians: 'Let them be accursed!' (1:8, 9) In one of his letters to the Corinthians he says that his opponents are ministers of Satan, disguising themselves as ministers of righteousness (2 Corinthians 11:15). To the church in Rome: 'Keep an eye on those who cause dissensions and offences, in opposition to the teaching you have learned; avoid them' (Romans 16:17). To the Philippians: 'Many live as enemies of the cross of Christ... Their end is destruction; their god is the belly; and their glory is in their shame; their minds are set on earthly things' (3:18, 19).

It may be that Paul is dealing with different problems and different groups of people in these letters; we cannot be sure that the troublemakers were all from the same source. What is certain is that in the churches to which Paul wrote (as far as the evidence has survived) there was trouble caused by conflicting ideas about the gospel and its implications. The letters that we have are the result of these disagreements. Had there been no conflict, there would have been no need for Paul to write in the way that he did.

The Lord of peace

Paul recognizes that the Thessalonian church will receive its peace from Christ—the Lord of peace. They are a church in God our Father and the Lord Jesus Christ (1:1). God had called them through the preaching of Christ by Paul, Silvanus and Timothy. Now God is using the authority of his agents to recall them into the grace and peace of Christ.

The situation was unstable; we have only these two letters to Thessalonica, and what can be pieced together from Paul's other letters and from the Acts of the Apostles. Had we been there at the time, we might well have been even more confused than we are now. One thing we would not have known then: would the church in the future follow Paul or would it follow his opponents? There is another difference between them and us: we know that Christ did not return from heaven as soon as some of them expected. But this is how it is: faith, not sight and certainty; charity, not rivalry and competition; hope, not possession.

PRAYER

Give peace to your church.
Renew us with your grace.
Show us your ways.

82

The LORD BE *with* ALL *of* YOU

A characteristic feature of many Christian liturgies is the exchange between the person presiding and the other members of the congregation. The president says, 'The Lord be with you', and they answer, 'And also with you.' There is a history behind this mutual prayer; it existed before it was incorporated into liturgical use.

In the book of Ruth, for example, Boaz greets the reapers in his field with, 'The Lord be with you', and they reply, 'The Lord bless you' (2:4). Similarly, in Judges, the angel of the Lord says to Gideon, 'The Lord is with you', and Gideon asks why, in that case, they are in such a poor way (6:12f.).

In Luke 1:28, the angel Gabriel greets Mary with the statement, 'The Lord is with you', and here, as in Judges and Ruth, 'Lord' refers to God the Father. The same will be the meaning of Paul's greeting to the Romans, 'The God of peace be with all of you' (Romans 15:33), and 'The God of peace will be with you' (Philippians 4:9). At the end of 2 Timothy, the formula is 'The Lord be with your spirit', and though it is uncertain whether this refers to Jesus or to the Father, scribes added 'Jesus' or 'Jesus Christ' to avoid the ambiguity.

In 2 Thessalonians 3:16, 'the Lord' probably means Jesus Christ, as in verse 18 below, where the prayer is that the grace of our Lord Jesus Christ may be with them; Christ is present where his grace is operative.

The word 'with' also is ambiguous. It can be used to mean 'with' in the local sense: alongside, in the midst of, in the same space as. But it can also be used to describe direction, purpose, intention, as in the saying, 'Whoever is not with me, is against me' (Matthew 12:30).

The presence of God

People in the ancient world do not seem to have taken space as seriously as we do, perhaps because the universe was assumed to be smaller than we think. God could be described as 'with' someone, even though he was believed to be in heaven; and the Christians apparently thought that there was no contradiction between saying that Jesus had been exalted to God's right hand, in fulfilment of

Psalm 110:1, 'The Lord says to my Lord, "Sit at my right hand until I make your enemies your footstool"', and saying that he lives in his agents on earth, as when Paul says, 'Christ... lives in me' (Galatians 2:20), or that the church is in Christ (as in the opening words of these two letters to the Thessalonians). When they thought about God, or Jesus, or the Spirit of God, they ignored the idea of space, distance, or absence in a literal sense.

To pray for God (or Christ) to be present with a congregation was to ask that those so addressed might be under the care, protection, guidance and influence of God (or Christ); that his will would be their will, and his goodness shared by all of them.

PRAYER

Thank you that there is room for you.
Let us not think we fill our space.
Be with us.

LITERALLY *or* SERIOUSLY?

As we reach the end of this short letter, we are bound to want to ask what we are meant to make of it. What is its meaning for us, living at the end of the second and beginning of the third millennium?

We think we can more or less understand it from a historical point of view: people were saying that the last days had arrived, and the letter was written to tell them that they had not, because there would be other events happening before the return of Christ. The restraining power of law and order would be removed; there would be the final rebellion against God, and the coming of the antichrist. In what sense are we to believe this?

It is possible to distinguish two ways of understanding these things, but it is not easy to name them: one might be called literal, the other serious, yet figurative.

A literal interpretation would say: Before Christ comes at the end of this age, these things will happen—chaos, rebellion, the antichrist. We shall know then that it is the final time, because these things are happening. But until these things happen, we are to wait, and we are not to identify the rebellion or the antichrist with any occasions or individuals in the history of the world.

The other interpretation of 2 Thessalonians takes what it says seriously, but not literally. It is not surprised if the quality of life for the majority of the world's inhabitants becomes more and more oppressive. The expectation is, according to this way of reading 2 Thessalonians, that life will become harder rather than easier, that faith in God will become more and more problematic, and that morality will decline rather than improve.

One problem with a literal interpretation is that, whenever it has been used in the past, subsequent events have always proved it wrong. Before 2 Thessalonians was written, some people thought that Antiochus IV (Epiphanes) was to be the final evil ruler and that God would take over the government of the world after his death. Later, in AD40, Gaius (Caligula), or later still, Nero or some other emperor, or Napoleon, Hitler, Stalin, Pol Pot, have been identified as the man of sin. But the end has not come.

To read 2 Thessalonians seriously but not literally is to give it a greater relevance to us today. Apocalyptic eschatology is always relevant. It makes it possible to hope against hope (Romans 4:18), to believe that God will bring good out of the worst evil and that he will sustain his people through the most chaotic times imaginable. It is the enemy of superficial optimism—the assumption that everything will continue to get better and better. It does not lead to despair, but to confidence in good works, because of God's power to raise the dead. Paul concludes his exposition of this theme with this exhortation: 'Therefore, my beloved, be steadfast, immovable, always excelling in the work of the Lord, because you know that in the Lord your labour is not in vain' (1 Corinthians 15:58).

PRAYER

Give us steadfastness.
Rescue us from the evil one.
Marana tha.

NOTES

NOTES

NOTES

NOTES

NOTES

NOTES

NOTES

NOTES

NOTES

NOTES

NOTES

NOTES

NOTES

NOTES

NOTES

GAL/THESS

THE PEOPLE'S
BIBLE COMMENTARY

VOUCHER SCHEME

The People's Bible Commentary (PBC) provides a range of readable, accessible commentaries that will grow into a library covering the whole Bible.

To help you build your PBC library, we have a voucher scheme that works as follows: a voucher is printed on the last page of each People's Bible Commentary volume (as above). These vouchers count towards free copies of other books in the series.

For every four purchases of PBC volumes you are entitled to a further volume FREE.

Please find the coupon for the PBC voucher scheme overleaf.

All you need do:

- Cut out the vouchers from the last page of the PBCs you have purchased and attach them to the coupon.

- Complete your name and address details, and indicate your choice of free book from the list on the coupon.

- Take the coupon to your local Christian bookshop who will exchange it for your free PBC book; or send the coupon straight to BRF who will send you your free book direct. Please allow 28 days for delivery.

Please note that PBC volumes provided under the voucher scheme are subject to availability. If your first choice is not available, you may be sent your second choice of book.

THE PEOPLE'S BIBLE COMMENTARY

VOUCHER SCHEME COUPON

[dashed box] [dashed box]

[dashed box] [dashed box]

TO BE COMPLETED BY THE CUSTOMER

My choice of free PBC volume is:
(Please indicate a first and second choice; all volumes are supplied subject to availability.)

❏ 1 and 2 Samuel
❏ Chronicles—Nehemiah
❏ Psalms 1—72
❏ Psalms 73—150
❏ Proverbs
❏ Nahum—Malachi
❏ Mark
❏ Luke
❏ John
❏ 1 Corinthians
❏ Galatians and Thessalonians
❏ James—Jude
❏ Revelation

Name: . . . .
Address: . . . .

. . . .
Postcode: . . . .

TO BE COMPLETED BY THE BOOKSELLER

(Please complete the following.
Coupons redeemed will be credited to
your account for the value of the
book(s) supplied as indicated above.
Please note that only coupons correctly
completed with original vouchers will
be accepted for credit.):

Name: . . . .
Address: . . . .

. . . .
Postcode: . . . .
Account Number: . . . .

Completed coupons should be sent
to: BRF, PBC Voucher Scheme,
Peter's Way, Sandy Lane West,
OXFORD OX4 5HG

Tel 01865 748227; Fax 01865
773150; e-mail enquiries@brf.org.uk
Registered Charity No. 233280

THIS OFFER IS AVAILABLE IN THE UK ONLY
PLEASE NOTE: ALL VOUCHERS ATTACHED TO THIS COUPON MUST BE ORIGINAL COPIES.